To Jay,

It has been a sincere
pleasure getting to know
you over the years! I hope
you enjoy the book. Look
forward to hearing your thoughts.

all my best,

THE BOOK OF
REAL-WORLD
NEGOTIATIONS

JOSHUA N. WEISS, PhD.

Cofounder, Global Negotiation Initiative at Harvard

THE BOOK OF
REAL-WORLD
NEGOTIATIONS

SUCCESSFUL STRATEGIES FROM
BUSINESS, GOVERNMENT, AND DAILY LIFE

Foreword by **William Ury,**
bestselling coauthor, *Getting to Yes*

WILEY

Published by John Wiley & Sons, Inc., Hoboken, New Jersey.

Published simultaneously in Canada.

For general information on our other products and services or for technical support, please contact our Customer Care Department within the United States at (800) 762-2974, outside the United States at (317) 572-3993 or fax (317) 572-4002.

Wiley publishes in a variety of print and electronic formats and by print-on-demand. Some material included with standard print versions of this book may not be included in e-books or in print-on-demand. If this book refers to media such as a CD or DVD that is not included in the version you purchased, you may download this material at http://booksupport.wiley.com. For more information about Wiley products, visit www.wiley.com.

Library of Congress Cataloging-in-Publication Data

Names: Weiss, Joshua N., author.
Title: The book of real-world negotiations : successful strategies from
  business, government, and daily life / Joshua Weiss , Ph.D.
Description: First Edition. | Hoboken : Wiley, 2020. | Includes index.
Identifiers: LCCN 2020028115 (print) | LCCN 2020028116 (ebook) | ISBN
  9781119616191 (cloth) | ISBN 9781119616160 (adobe pdf) | ISBN
  9781119616221 (epub)
Subjects: LCSH: Negotiation. | Negotiation—Social aspects. | Negotiation
  in business. | Negotiation—Cross-cultural studies.
Classification: LCC BF637.N4 W457 2020 (print) | LCC BF637.N4 (ebook) |
  DDC 658.4/052—dc23
LC record available at https://lccn.loc.gov/2020028115
LC ebook record available at https://lccn.loc.gov/2020028116

Cover Design and Images: Wiley

Printed in the United States of America

V10019880_071720

"Whosoever loves much performs much, and can accomplish much, and what is done in love is done well."

–Vincent Van Gogh

This book is dedicated to my wife, Adina. Thank you for loving me, letting me love you, and helping me do all the things I love to the best of my ability.

Contents

Foreword

I t is a great pleasure to introduce this remarkable book of negotiation stories compiled and analyzed by my old friend and colleague Joshua Weiss.

The Book of Real-World Negotiations helps fill a significant
gap in the negotiation literature. It complements the many
books in the field that introduce concepts, frameworks, and skills.
Here in this book, readers can learn not only about the creative
outcomes that are reached, but perhaps more importantly, *how*
the negotiators were able to achieve mutually satisfying results,
often against tremendous odds.

As an anthropologist, I appreciate the enormous power of
stories to convey lessons, cautions, and inspiration. The human
mind learns best through stories. Yet, because of sensitivities and
confidentiality, many of the best stories about negotiations are
rarely shared. This is where Joshua Weiss makes a real contribution. He has compiled a compelling range of negotiation stories
so that they can be discussed, analyzed, and learned from in a
way that only real-world cases can offer. Through these stories,
Weiss helps us understand the core principles and best practices
that can lead to success, as well as the details and nuances critical
to reaching agreement.

The book begins by highlighting business negotiations both
here in the United States and abroad, suggesting how negotiation can help parties overcome seemingly insuperable barriers to
agreement. Then Weiss leads us into negotiations in the world
around us – from political negotiations to working out disputes
in the nonprofit sector to hostage negotiation scenarios. In just

about every case, negotiators are required to delve deeply under the surface of the situation in order to discern what is really happening. Only by understanding this hidden dimension of the negotiation are they able to address the needs of their counterpart and reach a satisfactory solution. The key often appears to be the use of creativity, finding ways to expand the pie rather than just divvy it up.

Throughout these stories, Weiss also helps paint a picture of the hard work, tireless persistence, strategy, and creativity that goes into a successful negotiation – from preparation to key moments that shift the conversation to the factors that make an agreement stick.

With this compilation of inspiring case studies, Joshua Weiss has rendered a real service to the field of negotiation. I salute him and hope you, the reader, find much insight and benefit in the instructive stories that follow.

– William Ury

Preface

When I was first approached about writing a book, this is the one that immediately leapt to mind. Why, you might ask, was this so high on my list of things to write about? The rationale for the book and its focus is quite simple – there are a plethora of real-world negotiation success stories, in all walks of life, that convey critical lessons about effective negotiation. Unfortunately, most of those examples are hidden or never shared publicly, for various reasons. Thus, people are not learning from what has happened in the past to use in the future. These examples have much to teach us about what masterful negotiation looks like, and the world needs access to them.

What Am I Trying to Accomplish?

My belief, based on years of anecdotal evidence from a multitude of realms, is that there is a rather narrow and limited view of negotiation amongst the general public. Many laypeople believe negotiation is a win-or-lose endeavor that forces the parties to compromise on their essential goals. This perspective could not be further from the truth when it comes to successful negotiation. Instead of talking at people and trying to convince them that they are missing much of the promise that negotiation holds, I decided that I would rather try to demonstrate the value of negotiation through actual examples and let the reader make their own determination. The negotiations that follow hold invaluable teachings that are undeniable and will help to broaden people's perceptions on negotiation and how to overcome difficult obstacles and challenges that are often part of the process.

As such, this book will satisfy a need for real-world negotiation cases and solutions that exhibit effective negotiation. While there are certainly different examples embedded in other works in the field, there are very few books with a sole focus on case studies. This has happened for a good reason, which is that negotiators involved in these processes, or those privy to what has happened in different examples, are often not comfortable sharing the details due to confidentiality issues or other sensitivities. On this last point, many of the examples herein necessitated the changing of names so the negotiators cannot be identified. From my perspective, the actual names are not at all essential to the learning objectives. What is key to grasp are the lessons to be gleaned from these examples.

In addition to sharing these rare windows into the process and outcomes of various negotiations, certain lessons will be culled at the end of each scenario. While I will provide my own perspective on those lessons for discussion purposes, readers will certainly have the opportunity to decipher their own insights.

Who Am I Trying to Reach?

There are four groups of readers for this book. The first group is the lay public. Many people do not realize how much they negotiate on a daily basis, nor do they understand what really successful negotiation encompasses. It is my hope that, by reading these cases, people will come to understand the value of negotiation more fully.

The second group of readers are academicians who teach negotiation. There are an increasing number of negotiation classes in law schools, business schools, and other liberal arts programs at the university level and in high schools. Academicians and teachers will be able to use this book as an accompaniment to some of the more theoretical work that pervades the field.

The third group are students who take negotiations classes and who, I believe, will benefit greatly from real-world examples. These cases will help students to connect theory to practice and to imagine how they can use negotiation in their own careers.

Fourth and finally are trainers of negotiation. As the world changes and grows, most companies and organizations are coming to understand the critical importance of negotiation to their workplace. Whether it is internally or externally, most people are negotiating regularly and need to know how to do it as best as possible. The wide-ranging examples of negotiation in the book will also assist trainers in making different points and in helping participants envision what effective negotiation looks like practically.

How Is the Book Organized?

The book is broken into three broad sections based on the context in which these negotiations transpired. The first part covers domestic business cases, the second international business cases, and the third are cases from government and daily life. Each of these sections begins with an introduction and an overview of each of the cases to be covered within that section.

Introduction

The Power of Stories to Teach About Negotiation

"Storytelling is the most powerful way to put ideas into the world."
— Robert McKee, Professor[1]

"Tell me a story." That simple phrase has been at the heart of how conversations between people have begun for millennia and a significant vehicle for how knowledge is passed from one generation to the next. People have a knack for remembering stories, especially those with powerful lessons at their core.

Stories stemming from real-world negotiations are no different. In fact, actual negotiations that happen in business, government, and the world around us stay lodged in our memories better than theories, concepts, or facts. Why are these negotiation stories so powerful? An important part of the reason is because they often challenge our assumptions and preconceptions about what is achievable when people sit down together. As but one small example, consider the following story that a colleague shared with me a number of years ago.[2] It is conveyed from her point of view.

> Many years ago, I was hired as a negotiation advisor to help a small company with a merger they were seeking to engage in. Initially, I met with the company numerous times to prepare— discussing what their best-case scenario would look like (Aspiration Point), what they really hoped to achieve (Target Point), and at what point the deal no longer made sense and they would walk away (Reservation Point). All pretty standard notions. We also talked about the dynamics, such as power, that were involved in this situation. From our point of view the power issue was fairly balanced

between the parties given they were equal in size and net worth. As the negotiations drew closer, the company representatives asked that I sit in the room with them, away from the table, and give them advice during the breaks as the negotiation progressed. I had done this arrangement before, so I agreed.

As the negotiations began, both sides showed up with three negotiators as they had previously agreed. Almost immediately the other company's primary negotiator, named Oliver, took control and started to lay out the agenda in a *very* aggressive manner. He shared that they had run the numbers and that the offer they were putting on the table was more than fair. In particular, Oliver also claimed that they were bigger in size and brought more value to the table so they wanted control of the company after the merger. They would respect my client's company and their employees would all keep their jobs – for the time being. But that was the deal. Then Oliver said, "Take it or leave it."

Needless to say, this was not what we expected, but the team I had worked with knew enough that this was not acceptable to them – from both a process and an outcome perspective. The team tried to redirect the negotiation back to a problem-solving process. Oliver was not at all interested in that type of shift, even though it looked like his two colleagues were quite uncomfortable with the stance their team was taking. The two team members were shuffling papers, not making eye contact, and squirming in their seats in a noticeable fashion.

After a few minutes of back and forth with little progress Oliver started to take his papers and jam them, frustratedly, into his briefcase. He glared at our negotiators and simply said, "Well!" Our team said nothing. Oliver vaulted himself from the chair. The other two gentlemen looked puzzled, but began to pack up as well. Oliver, visibly annoyed, did not wait for them. He hurriedly marched across the room, opened the door, walked through it, and slammed it behind him. There was silence. Then laughter burst out from our negotiators and the other two men on the other side of the table. It turns out that Oliver, in his anger, had stormed right into a walk-in closet. But that was hardly the end of the story. Fifteen seconds passed. Then thirty seconds. Nothing happened. Oliver stayed in the closet.

Everyone's laughter turned to amazement the situation continued. After what I imagine was another 10 or 15 seconds, the door began to creak open. Oliver could hear the laughter. He sheepishly crept out of the closet with his proverbial tail between his legs.

One of our team members, named Kurt, regained control of himself and began to engage Oliver's two colleagues. Kurt explained to them that he could see a different way to approach the negotiation and would like to share it with their team. Oliver slinked back into the seat on the end. Before Oliver could reply, a member of his team learned forward and asked Kurt what he had in mind. Kurt explained a few different options, and the two other members of Oliver's team began to engage. Oliver sat on the sideline, not saying anything, eyes firmly planted on the floor.

After a few hours of productive back and forth, working through broad concepts and then the details, the parties were able to reach a tentative deal that was more balanced and reflected a true partnership. The merger eventually happened, worked well, and the new company is still thriving today.

There are many morals to this story. First, emotions, when not properly managed, can lead to big mistakes in negotiation. Interestingly however, in this case, they also led to a breakthrough. Thus, a second moral to be drawn from this story is that negotiation is inherently unpredictable, and anything can happen that can shift and move a process in unexpected ways. Approaching negotiations with a flexible and adaptable mindset, therefore, becomes another key takeaway. I am certain all the negotiators involved in this case will remember these lessons, and perhaps some others.

Coming back to negotiation stories in general, the stark reality is that there is not nearly enough public sharing of negotiation stories that exhibit the power of this process. Negotiations occur daily, but very few people know about them. Confidentiality and sensitive information often block the dissemination of these valuable lessons and anecdotes. However, if these stories are not shared, people won't be able to learn the vast potential of negotiation to forge new relationships, create productive deals, and resolve difficult conflicts.

There is a way to share these valuable stories, while shielding those who need to be protected. Some of the sensitive details found in negotiations are not critical in order to learn the lessons of how negotiators made their way through often improbable obstacles to reach creative solutions. The purpose of this book is to show you exactly *how* people went about doing this in their negotiations.

Why the Story Arc Is So Memorable for Negotiation

"There's always room for a story that can transport people to another place."

– J.K. Rowling[3]

Real-world stories are some of the best ways to learn and remember key ideas and concepts. Nary a person who hears the story of the negotiator and the closet and forgets it. For skeptics of negotiation, of which there are many, real stories are also very difficult to refute given that they *actually* happened.

The best stories have a memorable arc from beginning to end, overcoming obstacles, conflicts, and controversies, while ultimately conveying a lesson in an easy to understand manner. Let's briefly analyze these components to grasp why they are so compelling and leave an indelible mark in our memories. By doing this you will be able to identify these phases as you read the case studies.

As was mentioned, the best stories have an arc where the scene is set and the characters are introduced, the character's encounter a dilemma or problem to be overcome, and the characters usually land on a solution that very few saw coming. First, when it comes to the scene being set and the characters introduced, contemplate the *Harry Potter* series. The series begins with Harry's parents dying at the hands of Voldemort with only the infant, Harry, surviving. Harry's dilemma evolves into an epic conflict with Voldemort – good versus evil – that highlights the next part of any effective story.

Second, a story has to have a significant conundrum, dilemma, or conflict to overcome. This apex is where folklores and legends come from. Whether it is Pip in *Great Expectations* who desperately wants to be in the British upper class but is shunned, the tiny Hobbit Frodo Baggins in the *Lord of the Rings* who must undergo a virtually impossible journey to destroy the ring of power and save the world, or the simple and apparently meek shepherd boy David in *The Book of Samuel,* who improbably walks to the bottom of the Valley of Elah to fight the behemoth Goliath when nobody else will do so. This is the moment – unexpected and exhilarating – that keeps our attention and sets the stage for the culmination of the tale.

Third and finally is the finale, the sense of relief that the characters in the story come to a creative solution against all odds or a surprise ending that alters the way we think. The end – sometimes happy, sometimes not – is filled with lessons and morals that stay with us and teach us something that is unforgettable. Dorothy gets back to Kansas in the most improbable of ways, completing the *Wizard of Oz* saga in epic fashion and teaching us to look within for our strengths. Agatha Christie's *And Then There Were None* leaves us spellbound and surprised that the end was not all what we expected. Returning to *Harry Potter,* in the end Voldemort's demise is partly rooted in Harry himself and the inexorable connection they shared until the very end.

As you might imagine, negotiation stories, generally speaking, follow a similar pattern. They begin with an introduction, reach some kind of apex in terms of a quandary, and culminate with either a constructive way forward, the parties walking away to something else, or a stalemate. The connection between stories and negotiation is deeper, however. In difficult moments in negotiations we are much more likely to summon up a story with a happy or dramatic ending, a lesson or anecdote, than we are a concept or theory. In fact, according to Professor Jennifer Aker of Stanford Business School, stories are remembered up to 22 times more than facts alone.[4] Negotiation stories, simply put, stay with us and are easy to recall in critical moments.[5]

How to Read the Chapters: As Straight Case Studies or Puzzles to Be Solved

Given that this book is about these real-world negotiation stories, what is the best way to engage with them? Of course, there are a number of ways in which you can read the chapters. You can simply read them straight through and take in the background, preparation, negotiation, and lessons – looking for the aforementioned arc. By taking that approach you will see the natural progressions that negotiations often take, even if that progression is not always linear.

There is, however, perhaps another more interesting way to read the cases. Read the introduction, background, and preparation to the negotiation sections and then stop. Before reading further, ask yourself the following questions:

- Where do I envision this process heading, based on what I know?
- What impediments to the negotiation seem to be most critical to grasp?

- If I were one of the parties to this negotiation, where would I try to take this situation from this point forward? Why?
- What kind of creative solutions can I imagine based on what I know?

By approaching the cases in this interactive manner, they become negotiation puzzles to be solved and not just cases to be studied. Thinking through what you would do puts you in the role of the decision maker and highlights how challenging all of this can be to manage.

Organization of the Book and the Case Studies

While this book has a number of themes running through it that you will be able to identify, the cases have been grouped into three sections. The first group of cases are domestic business cases. These run the gamut through many different kinds of industries, but all the negotiations are situated within the United States. The second group of cases are international business examples. These have been separated out from the domestic cases primarily due to the cross-cultural elements that need to be managed as part of the negotiation and different norms that underlie the process. The third and final group of cases are from the public, or governmental, sector as well as the world around us. Each of the cases in this section have a very distinct character to them. While these situations are diverse in nature and cover some varied realms, all have something important to contribute to the overall story of negotiation.

Some of the cases in the book are straightforward negotiations between two or more parties. Other cases include the negotiating parties who are aided by a negotiation consultant or consulting firm. The prevalence of these external parties, who help negotiators reach solutions, has increased over the years and continues to grow due to their efficacy. Finally, the remaining cases involve a third party – a mediator, team of mediators, or facilitators – who also help the parties to reach a solution. These third parties serve less as advisors to one side and more as a process cop helping the negotiating parties to communicate more effectively and to solve difficult negotiation problems when they become entrenched in their positions.

Please also note that all of the cases in this book are from actual negotiation scenarios. This is not an edited volume in the traditional sense. The owners of the cases and examples were interviewed by the author, the cases were then written by the author, and then shared with the owners for accuracy purposes. You will note that some of the cases list the owners' names and others state that they were contributed anonymously. This approach was taken because some contributors had a desire for confidentiality and anonymity. When confidentiality was needed within the cases, the names of the people and the entities involved were changed. The lessons, however, are all very real and should help you develop your own negotiation solutions in the future.

Finally, there are a number of negotiation terms used throughout the book. For those familiar with negotiation, these terms will be commonplace and easily understood. For those who are new to negotiation and just learning the craft, there is a glossary at the end of the book that should be reviewed before reading the cases and then subsequently referred to as needed.

Notes

1. Quote can be found here: https://www.inc.com/dave-kerpen/you-need-to-become-a-better-storyteller-heres-some-inspiration.html
2. The colleague asked that the companies names be kept anonymous.

3. https://www.goodreads.com/quotes/54870-there-s-always-room-for-a-story-that-can-transport-people

4. For some very interesting research on the use of story in negotiation, see Rebecca J. Krause and Derek D. Rucker, "Strategic Storytelling: When Narratives Help Versus Hurt the Persuasive Power of Facts," *Personality and Social Psychology Bulletin*, 2019; featured in *Kellogg Insight* and *Wall Street Journal*. Krause and Rucker found that when a negotiator has a weak or moderate case, the use of a story to sway or compel the other is a powerful tool.

5. https://womensleadership.stanford.edu/stories

1

Mistakes Negotiators Make, and What Do Great Negotiators Do Anyway?

Learning to be an effective negotiator is a journey, not a destination. Along that journey you will encounter many notions about what effective negotiation looks like. Certain truisms about negotiation have come to the forefront as a result of the mistakes that people make. Similarly, with all the information out there and centuries of practice, we can also delineate what great negotiators do to solve some of the most difficult problems confronting humanity. Let's take a look at both of these before delving more deeply into the case studies.

Skepticism toward Negotiation, and Common but Inaccurate Myths

While we all negotiate regularly at work, at home, and in the world around us, negotiation still sometimes gets a bad name. Furthermore, there are some commonly held fictions related to negotiation that often lead people astray and away from creating the best deals or solutions possible. Below are the most common misperceptions of negotiation that are important to dispel from the outset.

A Winner and a Loser – and Nobody Wants to Lose

The first inaccurate belief about negotiation can be encapsulated in the memorable short story from Dr. Seuss, called "The Zax." To summarize the well-known tale, there once were a North-Going Zax and a South-Going Zax whose paths met. Neither Zax was prepared to move in deference to the other. They were both stubborn and prepared to stay where they were instead of giving the appearance, real or otherwise, that they would be the one to acquiesce to the other. The more they stood face to face, the more they tied their ego to their positions. They became entrenched. As the years came and went, so did progress, with highways and bridges built around them, and neither willing to budge. Alas, they spent the vast majority of their lives standing across from each other – both losing out.

Among the many lessons from this negotiation story is the belief that someone has to win and someone has to lose in a negotiation and neither party will budge if they are going to be the loser. This win-lose way of thinking leads people to conceive of negotiation from this vantage point – thereby limiting the negotiator's thoughts on what might be possible. This mindset often results in negotiators becoming ensconced in their positions – just like the two Zax. Stated differently, if a negotiator enters with this mindset then they will inevitably end up only looking for solutions that fit this type of outcome. While there are certainly some negotiations that may ultimately end up with a winner and loser to varying degrees, this misnomer pushes people to focus their attention in the wrong place and miss possible opportunities.

In addition, if a negotiator approaches their processes with this win-lose mindset, what impact does that have when they have to negotiate with the same people over and over again? Of course, they could always play the game of "I will win this time and next time it is your turn," but that approach is both illogical and produces poor agreements that leave value on the table and potentially creative solutions unexplored.

The False Promise of Compromise

The second mistaken – but commonly held – belief about negotiation is that the process hinges on a negotiator compromising something really important to them to get a deal done. Recall the famous story of King Solomon and the baby. One day two women came to King Solomon, and one of them said:

> "Your Majesty, this woman and I live in the same house. Not long ago my baby was born at home, and three days later her baby was born. Nobody else was there with us.
>
> "One night while we were all asleep, she rolled over on her baby, and he died. Then while I was still asleep, she got up and took my son out of my bed. She put him in her bed, then she put her dead baby next to me.
>
> "In the morning when I got up to feed my son, I saw that he was dead. But when I looked at him in the light, I knew he wasn't my son."
>
> "No!" the other woman shouted. "He was your son. My baby is alive!"
>
> "The dead baby is yours," the first woman yelled. "Mine is alive!"
>
> They argued back and forth in front of Solomon, until finally he said, "Both of you say this live baby is yours. Someone bring me a sword."
>
> A sword was brought, and Solomon ordered, "Cut the baby in half! That way each of you can have part of him."

"Please don't kill my son," the baby's mother screamed. "Your Majesty, I love him very much, but give him to her. Just don't kill him."

The other woman shouted, "Go ahead and cut him in half. Then neither of us will have the baby."

Solomon said, "Don't kill the baby." Then he pointed to the first woman, "She is his real mother. Give the baby to her."

Everyone in Israel was amazed when they heard how Solomon had made his decision. They realized that God had given him wisdom to judge fairly.[1]

King Solomon's example thankfully did not end in a gruesome compromise, but many negotiations do end up with a badly conceived compromise based on poor decision making. Many negotiators believe they must give up something of significant value to reach a deal. This belief is why many people dislike negotiating or feel anxiety during the process.

Frankly, while compromises might be needed from time to time, they certainly are not what effective negotiation is all about. It can be argued that compromising is a lazy approach to negotiation. Compromises usually happen when a negotiation becomes tense or a difficult issue remains elusive. The idea is to split the difference – with both being a little unhappy – so the parties can move forward.

So what do you do if you don't compromise? You resist the urge and dig into the issue in a deeper fashion. What that means is taking a creative approach where you explore all the underlying interests and sources of value that exist. When negotiators take this later approach, they often find they need not compromise because those interests and needs can be met in a multitude of ways. If, after exhausting all other avenues, they are left with no other option than to compromise, they can do so with confidence.

Misnomers about Manipulation and Deception

The third popularly held erroneous notion about negotiation is that it requires manipulation and deception. The thinking goes that when a negotiator finds something that creates discomfort in the other negotiator, they seek to exploit it. This view is all about taking advantage of the other negotiator. This approach also views the other negotiator as an adversary and treats them in that fashion.

The issue of manipulation and deception is another significant reason why so many people find negotiation disquieting. A series of studies have been conducted about comfort level and negotiation. One study in particular, from LinkedIn in 2012, found that only 40% of men and 26% of women were comfortable negotiating.[2] For people to become comfortable negotiating, they need to learn to let this conception of negotiation go and to realize that successful negotiation does not involve these deceptive tactics. In fact, it is really the opposite – building relationships and finding creative solutions – are what make effective negotiation possible.

The Strong Don't Negotiate

The fourth fallacious customary perception of negotiation is that it is for the weak. Strong people coerce others to do things, not persuade them. We often hear phrases such as "We don't negotiate with terrorists" or "Negotiation is about appeasement and not about standing up to the other." Think Chamberlain and Hitler. The reality is very different than that view. Negotiation is one of the key tools that we have at our disposal to solve our conflicts. There is nothing weak about this process.

Looking back through history, negotiation has been a critical tool to allow for human advancement and progress – from the Constitutional Convention of 1787 in the United States, to the

Cuban Missile Crisis in 1962 between the United States and the Soviet Union, to South Africa's National Peace Accord to end a decades-long conflict.[3] The problem is that most people are not conditioned to look to these milestones, but we must if we are to survive and grow as a species.[4]

Negotiators Are Born, Not Made

The fifth common myth is that negotiators are born and that negotiation is not something you can learn. As negotiation scholar Leigh Thompson reminds us, "I admit that I like Lady Gaga, but I think she has it wrong – at least when it comes to being a good (or great) negotiator. The truth is: I have never met a negotiator who was 'born this way.' The best negotiators I've met have been self-made, not manufactured by their parents."[5]

While people are indeed born with many traits that can help or hinder their negotiating ability, everyone can learn how to negotiate more effectively. Each person has their own negotiation ceiling that they can achieve, which requires time and effort. Furthermore, being an effective negotiator is not a destination, it is a journey. This means we are on that path forever – learning as we go and continually adding to our mindset and toolbox.

You Have to Sacrifice the Long-Term Relationship for Short-Term Gain

The final misguided conventional perception is that if a negotiator seeks to meet their short-term goals, they have to do so at the expense of the long-term relationship. The thinking goes that both can't be done; something has to give. This is a false dichotomy. Those that negotiate regularly, particularly with people with whom they have a long-term relationship, are always watching that fine line. They will never do something in the short term that damages the long-term relationship because they know it will come back to haunt them down the road. As J. Paul Getty reminded us, "You must never try to make all the money that's in a deal. Let the other fellow make some money too, because if you have a reputation for always making all the money, you won't have many deals."[6]

Moreover, the power of long-term relationships in negotiation is invaluable. When negotiators who have a strong relationship engage with each other, they are able to come up with the best deals possible. The reason for this is because they trust each other enough to share sensitive information and their underlying needs and interests that leads to finding hidden value. This is also true because when negotiators with a strong relationship hit a difficult snag in a process, they trust each other enough to persistently work together until they find a way forward. Without that type of relationship, fingers get pointed and blame gets heaped on the other.

What Great Negotiators Do: Five Key Principles

The case studies in this book demonstrate what effective negotiation really looks like in practice. Most readers will wonder, what is it, exactly, that great negotiators do so effectively? This question is often asked by many trying to learn this craft. Fortunately, the answer to what great negotiators do can be found in all of the cases collectively. As you read through the different cases, you will notice at least five principles emerging continuously. It is fair to say that these five tenets are a *necessary* condition for success in virtually all negotiations. If you use all of the principles below, you are much more likely to reach creative solutions that maximize the value in all your negotiations.

Principle 1: Invest in Preparation (Instead of Having a Plan)

There is no substitute for preparation, but people have to be careful how they prepare. Perhaps US president Dwight Eisenhower stated it best when he explained, "I have found that plans are useless, but planning is everything."[7] While Eisenhower was talking about preparing for war, the sentiment applies equally to negotiation, given the uncertainty involved and the fact that, as negotiators, we are always working with incomplete information. Even though it is very tempting for people, particularly those just learning to negotiate, to want to develop a specific plan of action, that approach rarely works effectively.

There are two reasons why plans are ineffective. The first reason is that what happens in a negotiation is partly contingent on the actions of the other. Since they are not reading from your playbook, they don't know what your plan is and, frankly, are not really interested in your plan. They are interested in their own approach and what will help them achieve their objective. The second reason is that negotiations are rarely linear and full of unexpected twists and turns. Given that truism, even the best-laid plans of negotiators are likely to go awry.

All that stated, engaging in broad-ranging contingency planning is extremely effective when it comes to negotiation (see Table 1.1).[8] Being clear on your end goal, but flexible on how to get there, is a critical component of successful negotiation. As many of the cases exhibit, this multipronged approach to preparation provides a negotiator with different avenues to go down in case one road is blocked.

Further, preparation provides negotiators with confidence to handle the ebbs and flows of a negotiation process. Just like studying for a test gives a person a level of confidence, so too does preparing for a negotiation. The more someone prepares, the more they can begin to envision the different avenues a

Table 1.1 Comparing Plans to Preparation.

A plan	Preparation
Is concrete	Is broad ranging
Has a specific objective	Has a specific objective
Uses a singular course of action on how to achieve the objective	Has many different avenues that one can go down to achieve an objective
Does not address what happens if people deviate from it	Is based on contingencies and enables the user to adjust to unforeseen circumstances
Assumes the landscape is clear and predictable	Assumes a lack of information and that the landscape is unpredictable

negotiation might go down, the interests of all involved, the myriad of options available, and how to handle unexpected inevitabilities.

Principle 2: Mindset and the Importance of Cultivating the Relationship

In all the cases in this book, one critical reason unique solutions were found was because of the mindset that at least one of the negotiators brought to the table. Mindset, while not readily apparent, underpins everything a negotiator does in a negotiation. For example, if a negotiator brings a mutual gains thought process to the table that puts them in the right frame of mind to envision potential solutions and to freely explore possibilities that meet both their and the other negotiator's needs.

This mutual gains mindset ties directly into the importance of relationship building. As Sir Francis Bacon reminded us, "In all negotiations of difficulty, a man may not look to sow and reap at once; but must prepare business, and so ripen it by degrees."[9] In other words, when a negotiator invests in a relationship, over the long term, the negotiations become easier and more fruit-ful. While most would not dispute the importance of cultivat-ing the relationship, some people feel they have to sacrifice the long-term relationship for a short-term gain. That is the exact opposite of what a negotiator should do. As has been previously expressed, one must seek to meet their short-term interests *while* preserving the long-term relationship. It is not easy to do, but it is indeed possible.

Furthermore, it is the relationship that will help you through difficult times and serious negotiation challenges. As my colleague William Ury has stated, "Investing in the relationship is like making a deposit in the bank of goodwill. There will be times in a negotiation when you need to make a withdrawal from that bank. If you have a strong relationship, you will be able to draw on those funds in the most important times."[10]

Principle 3: Creative Problem Solving

Negotiations, especially really difficult scenarios, require nego-tiators to envision the process as a creative problem-solving endeavor. In many of the cases herein you will notice that people had to engage in this type of thinking to uncover a possible but difficult-to-find solution. When a negotiator engages in creative problem solving, they free their mind from its traditional con-straints and are more able to engage in innovative explorations. These roads less traveled are often the avenues to success.

In order to problem-solve effectively, one has to see and make connections where others do not. These connections bring a new reality to the forefront and different workable ideas to light. Consider what William Plomer had to say about the crea-tive thinking process: "Creativity is the power to connect the seemingly unconnected."[11] When negotiators begin to see these elusive connections, they can solve even the most difficult of negotiation problems.

The reader should not, however, confuse problem solving with compromise. Many believe they are synonymous, but that could not be further from the truth. Compromise does not focus on creativity, but rather on finding a solution – usually a less than optimal one – and moving the negotiation forward. Compromise often yields to dynamics, such as time pressure and agreement bias (i.e. the strong desire to find a solution so all the parties can move on having gotten at least part of what they wanted).

Moreover, there is an inherent interconnected nature to negotiation. The reality is that, generally speaking, people in negotiation need each other. If they did not need each other they would just walk away. As one example of this, think about whether anyone has ever said to you in a negotiation, "Well, that is your problem. When you figure it out, let me know." It is my contention that people who say that really don't understand how negotiation works. This statement flies in the face of the aforementioned problem solving and fails to recognize that one negotiator needs the other to say yes so they can achieve their objectives and vice versa.

Principle 4: Managing the Emotional Side of Negotiation

For many years the conventional wisdom was that it was best for negotiators to keep their emotions out of the process. Remain calm and address the substance of the issues. While this may have seemed like reasonable advice, it proved not to be possible. Why? For one simple fact – human beings are both logical and emotional creatures.

As such, whether we like it or not, emotions always play a role in negotiation. As Christopher Voss reminds us, "Emotions aren't the obstacles to a successful negotiation; they are the means."[12] The question should not be whether to keep emotions out or let them in, but rather how does one let them in with some control? The way in which most negotiators do that today is through emotional intelligence.[13] In every negotiation case in the book, emotions played an important role and the negotiators did a very effective job of bringing their emotions to the table with some restraint. In addition, in these cases the negotiators involved managed not only their own emotions well, but were also, at times, called on to manage the emotions of their negotiation counterparts so that their emotions did not overwhelm them and become an impediment to success.

	Personal Competence	***Social Competence***
Awareness	Self-Awareness • Emotional Self-Awareness *Recognizing and understanding our own emotions*	Social Awareness • Empathy • Organizational Awareness *Recognizing and understanding the emotions of others*
Actions	Self-Management • Achievement Orientation • Adaptability • Emotional Self-Control • Positive Outlook *Effectively managing our own emotions*	Relationship Management • Conflict Management • Coach and Mentor • Influence • Inspirational Leadership • Teamwork *Applying our emotional understanding in our dealing with others*

Principle 5: Uncovering the Hidden Dimensions of Negotiation

In every case study you will read about the hidden dimensions and underlying interests involved in the respective negotiations. These veiled elements require skill to notice and to grasp how they are impacting the process. Many of the covert dimensions of negotiation are far from obvious and require a lot of exploration and investigation. For example, in some of the cases there were cross-cultural elements impacting the process and the thinking of the participants.

Astute negotiators look for these dimensions and assume there is more going on than meets the eye. In other cases there are key psychological dimensions involved, such as face saving, that underpin the entire process. Finally, in still other examples, there are critical interests or needs that are driving the process, but are lurking under the surface like the hidden elements of an iceberg.

Notes

1. Kings 3:16–28, Contemporary English Version.
2. Casserly, M. "Why American Women Lose at Negotiation – And What We Can Do about It," *Forbes* April 3, 2012; https://www.forbes.com/sites/meghancasserly/2012/04/03/why-american-women-lose-negotiation-linked-in-career/#171f3577ac45

3. For more examples, please see Fredrik Stanton, *Great Negotiations: Agreements that Changed the Modern World* (Yardley, PA: Westholme Publishing, 2010).

4. For a comprehensive read of how negotiation and conflict has been resolved throughout history, see William Ury, *The Third Side: Why We Fight and How We Can Stop* (Penguin Books, 2001).

5. Thompson, L. "Masters of Negotiation: Born This Way?" Kellogg News. https://www.kellogg.northwestern.edu/news_articles/2014/12052014-made-not-born.aspx

6. Quotation can be found at https://theamericangenius.com/entrepreneur/19-inspirational-quotes-on-the-art-of-negotiation/

7. Quote can be found here: https://www.azquotes.com/quote/358520

8. "The Paradox of Planning," https://www.breakingthewheel.com/paradox-of-planning/. A helpful analogy here might be how one prepares for chess. The grand masters tend to think more in contingencies than one concrete plan or approach.

9. Quote can be found here: http://www.literaturepage.com/read/francis-bacon-essays-99.html

10. Interview with William Ury, August 26, 2019.

11. Quote can be found here: https://www.brainyquote.com/quotes/william_plomer_404671

12. Quote can be found here: https://www.brainyquote.com/topics/negotiation-quotes

13. For more on the core tenets of emotional intelligence, see works by Daniel Goleman.

I

Domestic Business Cases

"The most critical thing in a negotiation is to get inside your [counterpart's] head and figure out what he really wants."[1]

– Jacob Lew

Business in the United States is ripe with endless opportunities to negotiate. Whether it is internally with bosses, colleagues, or employees, or externally with clients, partners, or contractors, negotiation is ubiquitous. Many of these negotiations include a financial aspect to them, but there are almost always other issues that are part of the equation. Furthermore, the challenge for any negotiation in a business context is how to meet your short-term needs *while* also building the long-term relationship. Businesses are sure to fail if they sacrifice the short term for the long term and vice versa.

When I ask the companies and organizations I work with how many of their negotiations are one-time encounters compared to negotiating with the same people time and again, the responses are approximately 15% for one-time encounters and 85% for continual negotiations.[2] As one CEO commented to me a few years back, "Our best new customers and source of revenue are our current clients. How we negotiate with them is critical to the relationship and whether they stay with us over the long term. If we seek to squeeze every dollar out of every deal we will indeed do better in the short term, but we will lose in the long term. I have seen clients leave because of a negotiation process where they felt disrespected or how a lopsided agreement in our favor made them feel after the fact. It is simply not worth it to our company, or our bottom line, to take that approach."[3]

What you will notice when you read through all of these cases is that there are a lot of different types of topics being negotiated. Observe the differences but also the similarities that cut across the examples.

Part 1 presents seven cases for you to read, consider what is happening and how a solution was reached, and try to understand the lessons involved. As you read, see if you can spot the places where some of the principles that make negotiators great that were previously mentioned apply. While these are not spelled out in the chapters themselves, they are embedded within the examples if you are looking for them.

The first case focuses on a negotiation between two companies – Amity and Branco – that had recently merged. Initially the negotiated merger progressed without complication. Once the deal had been finalized, however, some of Amity's people (the larger of the two companies) began to assert their dominance and to seek changes that would benefit them. Quickly the situation began to turn sour and it seemed as if the newly merged company was going to have significant turmoil from within. Through some creative thinking and unique accounting measures based on underlying interests developed by an employee at Branco, the situation was dramatically altered and a solution was found that benefitted all.

The second case stems from a productive relationship between two companies – Blue Planet Recycling and Plastics Be Gone. They had worked together very well for three years and a renegotiation was in the offing. The renegotiation transpired in a very productive fashion. So, you might be wondering, what is this case all about then? The answer is that there was room to make the agreement between the parties even better and the negotiators did not realize that possibility until the author, as an outside consultant, brought the opportunity to their attention.

The third example is about a negotiation to rework the relationship between two very large companies. The first company, Zazas, is a well-known retail convenience store that sought to renegotiate with Loguserve, its primary wholesaler and distributor. While they had worked together for over twenty years, they had a relationship that could best be described as functional, but difficult. The negotiation centered around Zazas wanting to move away from a sole supplier arrangement with Loguserve, as well as Zazas wanting to insource numerous dimensions of their business. While not an easy task, a successful solution was found due to the help of an outside consulting firm, some very effective preparation, and one side putting themselves firmly in the shoes of their negotiation counterpart.

The fourth case is a negotiation over a failed acquisition between a very large company called Mantosar and a smaller company called Contrexo. While the acquisition did occur, the principals at Contrexo shortly thereafter became very unhappy and wanted to buy their company back. A costly lawsuit loomed over the subsequent negotiation process – as Contrexo tried to get out from under the deal. In the end, a strong relationship enabled the parties to steer away from a destructive lawsuit – even though that course of action made some sense for one of the parties involved – and to reach an agreement that was ultimately better for both parties.

The fifth case hinged on the concept of indemnification and the underlying element of risk involved for the respective parties. A law firm involved in the case, Pine and Whitney, was concerned about their liability, while the other firm, DOAR, who had worked with Pine and Whitney before and had no previous issues related to indemnification, struggled to understand the hidden dilemma. DOAR was on the verge of exercising their BATNA and walking away, when they stopped themselves, revisited the situation, and came up with a much better creative solution that met the needs of all involved and enabled them to proceed with the relationship.

The sixth case required a very delicate balance between the short- and long-term negotiation needs of the companies involved. One company – AL Recovery – had short-term needs with the potential to lose out on long-term opportunities. The other company, Rambling Recyclers, was serving as an agent for a much larger company called Savory Grain Products. Rambling Recyclers had to manage both their short-term goals and seek a way to create a new long-term relationship between themselves and AL Recovery. As that new relationship was being formed in a different context, some difficult decisions needed to be made by Rambling Recyclers. Part of the challenge for Rambling Recyclers required setting a firm reservation point and not going beyond it. That led to Rambling Recyclers exercising their BATNA and demonstrating to AL Recovery that they were willing to walk away from a deal that simply did not work for them. Ultimately, by walking away from one deal, Rambling Recyclers sent an important signal about what they were not willing to do and establishing their credibility. AL Recovery and Rambling Recyclers did find their way back to the table and took steps toward a new and productive relationship under different, but mutually satisfactory, terms.

The seventh case in this section is a classic example of a behind-the-scenes figure in a negotiation who was *really* calling the shots. A consultant, called Engineering Experts Inc., was working with a client, Amity County, on a complex engineering project. The parties unexpectedly hit a snag and needed to negotiate a way forward. Initially that way forward was blocked until a person, literally sitting behind the Amity County representative and providing him advice, came out from the proverbial shadows.

When that happened, a window was opened to what was really bogging down the process. Once that clarity was achieved, a mutually acceptable solution was not far behind.

Notes

1. Quote can be found here: https://www.azquotes.com/quotes/topics/negotiation.html
2. Of course, this will vary depending on the industry, but generally across the board these statistics hold true.
3. Conversation with the CEO of a client that wished to remain anonymous.

2

Saving a Merger
with Creative Thinking

Anonymous contribution

Mergers are a very interesting challenge when it comes to negotiation. Not only do you have to negotiate the terms of the merger itself but, perhaps more importantly, you also have to handle the continual negotiations that transpire as the agreement gets implemented and the new organization takes form. Among the many difficulties that need to be dealt with are differing organizational cultures, position eliminations and recalibrations, and sometimes an imbalance of power between the merging organizations. These are not easy to address and can hamper the new organization for months, and even years, to come.

As the organizations settle into their new reality, they must navigate tricky waters. When doing so, the dividing lines between the previous organizations can last for quite some time until new working relationships form across those traditional lines. In the case that follows, all of the aforementioned dynamics were on display. Fortunately, these challenges were juxtaposed with some creative thinking that saved the new entity from a potentially debilitating conflict.

Background and the Negotiation Challenge

Two companies, called Amity and Branco, had recently agreed to merge. As they were working through some of the issues post the merger, an unexpected twist arose. Amity abruptly changed one of their policies and decided to "tax" each division in a new way that would cost Branco a whopping $25 million. The tax was supposed to cover the costs of harmonizing the two firms' computer systems and other technologies. Amity felt it could do this because it was the much larger of the two companies and the one doing the acquiring. As such, it decided to throw its weight around before the dust had settled.

The tax on Branco was so onerous that it would turn the economics of the merger upside down, making it a financial loser for Branco. Needless to say, frustration levels from employees at Branco rose quickly. Two of the people at Branco who were deeply involved were Danny and his boss, Amy, both of whom were stunned at the turn of events and worried about their jobs and the jobs of their colleagues. Upon hearing the news Amy quickly degenerated into a funk and was trying desperately to figure out how to salvage the situation. Danny did the only thing he could think of – he rolled up his sleeves and started tossing around ideas in his head about how to tackle the problem.

Preparing to Negotiate

As Danny racked his brain, searching for answers, he recalled a negotiation course he had taken as part of his Master of Business Administration (MBA) degree. He began to work his way through the process he learned, represented by the acronym I FORESAW IT, which lists ten questions a negotiator should ask and answer by way of preparing for a negotiation. The questions are as follows:

I for Interests: What are the underlying interests and needs that the parties have?

F for Factual research: What research can be done by way of preparation?

O for Options: What possible creative options exist in the negotiation?

R for Rapport, Reactions, and Responses: What tone will you set for the negotiation with the other, what worrisome reactions will the other side likely have to your ideas, and how will you respond?

E for Empathy and Ethics: Do you really understand the needs of the other?

S for Setting and Scheduling: Where and when will you hold the negotiation?

A for Alternatives: What are some of the things each side might do if you cannot reach agreement?

W for Who: Who can influence the talks?

I for Independent Criteria: What independent criteria can you point to that will help you in your negotiation?

T for Topics, Targets, and Tradeoffs: What topics will you discuss, what are your targets in this negotiation, and what tradeoffs are you willing to make?

Danny immediately began doing intense factual research – one of the first steps in the process. With some information already at the ready, he asked to meet with Amy. Danny listened to her concerns and frustrations about the current situation and then slowly began to walk her through the I FORESAW IT framework, asking questions about the interests at stake, and the factual and financial aspects. As the process wore on, Amy's mood began to change from frustration to hope. She called in two other colleagues from Branco to participate. Together, they used Danny's research and developed a number of possible options on how to move forward. As Danny recounted, "It was great to have some bad ideas. . . it made the ultimate suggestion stand out."[1]

As they continued their way through the rest of the I FORE-SAW IT framework, Danny recalled "we realized something obvious that everyone had missed when the two sides were bickering (i.e. taking positions) during the negotiation. If we didn't integrate the technologies, the costs to the firm would actually go up! We had the right to block the integration. Why? Because my company would be forced to maintain a myriad of duplicate systems, which would create serious inefficiencies. I realized we had a common interest I could highlight."[2] That common interest was cost savings.

The solution Amity and Branco ultimately found was a result of questioning assumptions and digging deep for a solution no one had thought of based on a special accounting method. Amy and Danny's division would pay its portion of the costs to change the system, but it wouldn't pay the current operating costs. The method would also cut costs to other divisions by ending duplicate accounting systems and wouldn't create any further financial issues for either side. Danny concluded that he would wind up saving $14 million for both sides using this approach, salvaging the merger, reviving his and his boss's careers, and winning the respect of his new colleagues. "I was hero for a day," he added.[3]

But how did Danny actually negotiate this outcome into being?

The Negotiation

There were really three sequential negotiations in this case. The first was the original merger that defined the terms under which the two companies would come together. The agreement was vague and general enough that it left open the possibility of such a tax, among other things.

The second negotiation was the positional back and forth that was going on between the parties during the implementation. Amity wanted the tax and Branco was vehemently opposed to it. In all the squabbling and positional posturing, a potential solution lay under the surface, but nobody had found it because they were not looking for it. This is a common problem in primarily positional negotiations and why they often yield inefficient agreements that leave possible solutions and hidden value undiscovered.

The third negotiation emerged after Danny, Amy, and their colleagues were able to move beyond positions to interests and flesh out the aforementioned underlying solution. The reality was that there was not much to negotiate after that solution was found by Danny and colleagues in the preparation phase. The solution not only unstuck the negotiation, but cleverly met the underlying needs of all the parties better than the proposed tax that would have hurt Branco and severely damaged the relationship.

Lessons Learned

There are a number of key lessons here that require further analysis and elucidation. Many of the lessons hinge on preparation and looking beneath the surface for answers.

Lesson 1: The Power of Preparation

The first lesson is the value of preparation and learning from a clear framework in order to do so. Danny had learned the I FORESAW IT framework in a negotiation class and was smart enough to recall it and use it to analyze the situation anew. It would have been very easy for Danny to join in on the pessimism his colleagues were feeling and to start looking for another job. However, he resisted that temptation and thought differently about the negotiation problem in front of him. Not only that, but he was able to effectively demonstrate how this would work to his colleagues as well as the other party.

Lesson 2: Making the Shift from Positional to Interest Based

The second lesson was the key shift from a positional, back-and-forth negotiation, to a more interest-based way of viewing the situation. Instead of getting pulled into the game of one-upmanship, Danny stepped back and searched for a creative solution. This was not initially apparent to Danny and required some important research into the nuances of the tax and why it was being levied. Once Danny uncovered the solution, all he had to do was frame the issue in the right manner for both parties. He did that with a focus on the common interest of cost savings.

Lesson 3: Creativity Can Level the Negotiation Playing Field

The final lesson is that even in the face of a power asymmetry, you have options if you think creatively enough. Amity decided to throw its weight around as the merger was just getting solidified. Had the tax gone forward, it is quite likely that the merger either would not have survived or would have been far less profitable. Danny and his colleagues were not daunted by this power imbalance and were able to break the problem down in such a way that nullified the power involved and forced Amity to come to their senses.

Notes

1. Interview with anonymous submitter done in the year 2000.
2. Interview with anonymous submitter done in the year 2000.
3. Interview with anonymous submitter done in the year 2000.

3

Congratulations, You Reached Agreement. Now Can You Make It Better?

Contributed by Joshua N. Weiss

Professor Howard Raiffa of Harvard Business School developed an innovative concept called Post Settlement Settlement.[1] While it seems like a bit of an odd name, the idea is brilliant and rather simple. After the parties to a negotiation reach an agreement, they normally progress to the implementation phase as the next step in the process and move quickly toward putting the agreement into practice. Raiffa, however, suggests that the parties pause and consider another step before rushing off to implement the agreement.

The additional Post Settlement Settlement step Raiffa advocates for hinges on the parties asking each other a simple question: "Is there any way that we can make this agreement better for *both of us*?"[2] Somewhat surprisingly, when negotiators take the time to revisit their agreements in the way Raiffa counsels, they often uncover assumptions they made and other areas of interests that were left unexplored. This new information leads to additional places of value that were left out of the original agreement and an expanding of the pie. As a result, both sides gain even more than the already acceptable initial agreement they came up with together. Let's see how this concept works in practice.

Background and the Negotiation Challenge

A number of years ago I was working with a recycling company called Blue Planet Recycling (BPR), which was based in the midwestern part of the United States. BPR had approximately two hundred employees with a head office and a few regional offices in the Southwest and West. I was there to conduct a negotiation training for 75 people at the headquarters, but the training turned into something much more for a few participants.

At one of the coffee breaks I was talking to two associates, Zena and James. They were in charge of negotiating the renewal of a contract with one of their biggest suppliers, Plastics Be Gone Inc. (PBG). BPR and PBG had recently finished a successful partnership and had just verbally agreed to another contract. Naturally Zena and James were thrilled and were feeling pretty good about what had transpired. Then I started asking them some questions, and they realized there was a new opportunity to be explored that they had not previously considered.

Preparing to Negotiate

"Were the terms the same as the previous contract?" I queried. "Why yes, they were, and they work well for both of us" was the reply from Zena, who was brimming with pride. "That is terrific," I responded. Then I continued, "Did you ask if there was any way that you could improve upon the original agreement?" The two of them looked at me quizzically. "Um, no," James stated a bit sheepishly, "why would we? It was a good deal. We figured we would just replicate it."

"Well, that's okay, but let me ask you, did you all sign on the dotted line yet?" I nudged a bit further. Zena immediately began to see where this was going, perked up, and said, "Actually, no we have not. We have just agreed in principle. Do you think we could still explore what you are talking about?" I smiled. "Why not? Let's talk about what you might discuss. There is really one simple question to ask: Is there any way in which we might make this agreement better from your perspective?" They both nodded. "Oh, but that is not all. You need to think about what else would be of value to you that you could ask for in return. For example, if you could lengthen the contract, would that help you? What about changing the payment schedule so it happened at a different time in the quarter? Things along those lines." James and Zena looked at each other and smiled. They grabbed their lunch and hurried off to a table nearby to discuss the possibilities at some length. A little while later I looked over and they had a flip chart with two columns clearly delineated. The first column was additional things the supplier might want, and the second column was what they could ask for in return.

Before the training started up again an hour later, Zena and James came back over to show me what they had done. They had come up with a number of BPR's possible interests that they had not explored that would bring some added value. Similarly, they also flipped the conversation around and brainstormed some options related to a number of unexplored areas the representatives of PBG might consider. They came up with these possibilities by thinking about some objective criteria that had been included in previous agreements with other companies, but that were not part of the original agreement with PBG.

After another few hours of training I finished up and headed home. Before doing so, I spoke to Zena and James about what they had created. It seemed as if they had come up with some interesting possibilities. I asked them to let me know what happened after they reengaged. They told me they would make sure to keep me informed.

The Negotiation

Approximately a week later I received an email with the subject line "Wow thanks!" The email was from both Zena and James and they went into some detail about what occurred in their Post Settlement Settlement negotiation. In essence, they had a very productive conversation with the supplier's representative, Anwar. When they initially contacted Anwar and asked the question we discussed, Anwar replied, "That is the first time anyone has ever asked me that. Let me think about it." As the two recounted in the email, "At that point we looked at each other and smiled. We knew we were onto something and there might be a real possibility of making the agreement better."

They went on to explain that Anwar called them back the next day and asked that they increase the length of the contract to three years. He shared that having the longer contract helps them do their projections into the future and creates more stability for them. Further, Anwar asked if they could make their payments in the middle of the month instead of at the end for cash flow purposes. Anwar elucidated that having the ability to spread these payments out would really be of help to them on a number of fronts.

Zena and James thought these two changes would be acceptable, but they took the request to their boss to verify and discuss what they might ask for in return. It turned out that the length of the contract was a shared interest that would also benefit BPR.

They did not think that three years would be in PBG's interest, but it turned out to be an assumption Zena and James made. Further, BPR did not have an issue with the change of payment date – they actually had a similar cash flow challenge to manage that occurred for them at the end of the month.

Zena and James then turned their attention to what they might ask for from Anwar as part of the enhanced deal. After discussing what else they might secure with their boss, they determined that if they could change the monthly pickup date to earlier in the month it would help them with their refuse and recycling plan and to manage their overall operations more effectively.

Zena and James then got back on the phone with Anwar. They discussed all of these things and the change to the monthly pickup date. The change would require a bit of reworking, but Anwar was willing to do it because he was getting additional things he needed. He agreed to take this back to his boss to see what she would say about the changes.

A week later they had a new and improved agreement in place and the relationship has continued to grow and flourish since then.

Lessons Learned

The takeaways embedded within this case are copious. The keys here were not to be satisfied with what came before, but rather to keep looking for value and ways to make a previously good agreement even better.

Lesson 1: Maximizing Value

First, creative ideas, such as Post Settlement Settlement, provide the opportunity for negotiators to make certain they are maximizing all the value to be had in their negotiations. Sometimes negotiators feel compelled to reach an agreement quickly, thereby missing opportunities to determine all the interests and needs involved. Before concluding any agreement, always ask: Can we make this better for both of us?

This also requires the negotiators to really think hard about what would bring them value and to be open to the other side doing so as well. As we witnessed in this situation, when the negotiators slowed the process down, checked their assumptions, and conducted a thorough examination of all the things they value, they were able to make the agreement better.

Lesson 2: Don't Let Past Agreements Dictate Future Arrangements

Second, in this example one can see the problem of past agreements dictating future behavior. Originally, Zena and James were satisfied with an agreement that replicated what had been done in the past, thereby missing potential opportunities for a better deal. It is easy to fall into this way of thinking and to think a good agreement is, well, good enough.

The key to avoiding this problem is to approach each negotiation as a separate and distinct process. Recognize that while some things are the same, there are very likely to have been things that have changed since the last agreement. Put differently, examine the situation for similarities and differences. Further, whatever assumptions you are making about the process need to be checked with the other party and thought through carefully.

Lesson 3: Simple Questions Can Unlock Complex Issues

The third lesson is that simple questions are sometimes the best and most powerful. Negotiators can outsmart themselves with excessively complicated questions and analysis, when a simple and straightforward question will often suffice. Try to think of questions that go right to the heart of the issue and how best to frame them so the other will hear it and genuinely consider what you are asking. This may require some preparation and trying out questions on friends or colleagues to hone them effectively.[3]

Lesson 4: Added Value Needs to Be There for All Parties

Finally, in order to make this Post Settlement Settlement process work effectively, both sides have to find some value that was left covered. If only one party identifies an issue that will benefit them, this process will not work. While this might seem like a significant roadblock, it is actually not that problematic if the parties think long enough and inject some creativity into the process.

Notes

1. Raiffa, H. "Post-Settlement Settlements," *Negotiation Journal* 1:1 (January 1985). For an excellent additional analysis of Post Settlement Settlement, see R. Mendenhalt, "Post Settlement Settlement: Agreeing to Make Resolutions Efficient," *Journal of Dispute Resolution* 1 (1996).
2. Please remember that the key to Post Settlement Settlement is that the agreement has to be made better for all the parties, not just one.
3. Please note that when working cross culturally, you need to be careful with the kinds of questions you ask. In some cultures, such as the US, direct, clear, concise questions are appropriate. In some other countries, such as Japan, a more indirect approach and set of questions would be necessary.

4

You Want What? How to Negotiate Significant Changes to a Relationship – without Destroying It

Based on an interview with Vantage Partners

Anytime there is a negotiation that happens within the context of a long-term relationship, issues are bound to arise. That is even the case when the relationship is productive. It is that much more difficult when the relationship is already difficult and significant changes are being proposed by one entity toward the other. Then add in the dimension of many billions of dollars at stake and the parties need to walk a very fine line to find a deal that will remake the relationship and that still works for all the parties participating.

Such was the situation in the example below. What ultimately helped the parties to get to a new and different place was that one party had a well-defined negotiation strategy, and the discipline to follow it – adapting to the other party's actions, versus simply reacting. Common wisdom is that it "takes two to tango" but this case study shows the power just one party can exert to shape negotiations in a positive way. External forces also helped nudge the parties in a positive direction.

Background and the Negotiation Challenge

The first party to this negotiation is a large retail chain, with thousands of stores across the United States, called Zazas. The second party to the negotiation is a wholesaler and logistics service provider, called Loguserve.

Zazas and Loguserve had worked together for over 20 years. The relationship was fairly contentious, with a decent amount of distrust, dislike, and tension. The business between the two entities was substantial, with Zazas heavily dependent on Loguserve for much of what was stocked in its stores, while Loguserve was also dependent on Zazas for a significant percentage of their revenue. As an example of the depth of the relationship, in any of Zazas locations, well over 75% of the items were supplied by Loguserve. Without them, Zazas did not really have a business.[1]

With such an intricate level of connectedness in their businesses, why was the relationship so strained? A key part of Zazas business model is making certain that whatever a customer wants is on their shelves. They target a 99% stock rate – meaning it is exceedingly rare that an item gets stocked out and is not on the shelves. This aspiration puts them at odds with Loguserve's needs because wholesale distribution tends to work best at a maximum of a 95% stock rate. The basic logic of this is that once a business goes from 95% to 96% to 97%, the cost with each percentage starts to curve significantly upward. A great deal of safety stock is required to get above a 95% stock rate, and that swells storage – as well as increasing the likelihood that products will go to waste (either because the items are perishable, or the item becomes obsolete due to rapidly changing consumer tastes). Such waste is very costly.

This is not just about charging Zazas more from Loguserve's perspective. The reason Loguserve can provide this type of distribution at lower cost is because they are scaling their warehousing, trucks, and logistics infrastructure over many different companies. Another strain on the relationship comes from delivery schedule. Zazas is constantly complaining that deliveries are not on time or come during peak hours. Loguserve wants the freedom to deliver whenever it fits their schedule, to maximize delivery route efficiencies.

On top of this tension, there were a few different problems related to the complicated nature of the contracts Zazas and Loguserve had signed in the past. These problems ultimately manifested themselves in Zazas accusing Loguserve of intentionally providing them with false data, and overcharging them based on that false data. Zazas caught the discrepancies, and Loguserve eventually made financial recompense, but the question that was never answered was whether this was an honest mistake, as Loguserve claimed, or whether Loguserve was trying to take advantage of Zazas and got caught. Zazas was convinced it was the latter, but the air was never cleared, and trust was never repaired.

Lastly, due to the significant nature of the business relationship, every time a problem arose the leaders of both companies tended to let their emotions get the better of them and the issues that could have potentially been solved ended up escalating. Each time this happened the relationship became more adversarial and confrontational. Efforts at difficult conversations were handled poorly, further exacerbating the distrust and dislike.

Given the state of the relationship and the desire to make significant and complicated changes, Zazas reached out to Vantage Partners – a consulting firm with deep expertise in complex negotiations – to assist with the restructuring of the relationship, and resultant renegotiation of a new contract. Zazas explained to the partners at Vantage that there were two years left on their current contract and they wanted to renegotiate substantially different terms in the new agreement. They shared the backstory of the difficult relationship and that past negotiations had been very adversarial in nature. Zazas also explained that they had a set of objectives that were important to achieve, but it was going to be very difficult to get Loguserve to agree.

Preparing to Negotiate

The changes that Zazas wanted to make were numerous and significant. First, they wanted to make improvements to Loguserve's service levels – on-time delivery to stores, better fill rates, and better delivery time windows. Second, given they are in a low-profit-margin business, Zazas wanted these improvements but didn't want to pay more for them. Third, although Loguserve had been the primary supplier, Zazas' board of directors wanted them to diversify suppliers, and also to begin to build the capabilities to do some work internally (like demand forecasting) that they had historically relied on Loguserve to do. There was simply too much risk in being so dependent on one supplier. So Zazas wanted to bring in another supplier and initially shift 5 to 10% of their business to them with more being shifted in the future. To sum up, Zazas wanted better service, lower pricing, and to take some business away from Loguserve in the short term and even more business over time. To top it off, the secondary wholesaler Zazas thought they would likely select was Loguserve's biggest and most hated competitor!

In the longer term, Zazas wanted to change their whole business model and purchase more directly from bigger consumer brands that actually produced the items they stocked in their stores. To this point, Loguserve had not only done the supplying and delivery, but also the purchasing and category management. Over the next 7 to 10 years Zazas wanted to build their own demand forecasting, category management, and own their own purchasing. Over these many years they ultimately wanted to rely on Loguserve just to do logistics, warehousing, and delivery. Zazas longer-term trajectory, therefore, was to insource a lot of things and take away a big chunk of business from Loguserve.

Zazas' team met with the Vantage team to work through how best to approach all of these changes. It was very clear to all involved that the negotiations were going to be exceedingly difficult. One of the first questions from Zazas to Vantage was about when to share the longer-term trajectory change – was it best to do that up front, later, or to withhold that information? The Vantage team advised that it would be critical to come clean from the outset, not only for reasons of business integrity (which was Zazas' inclination) but also because such information was almost certain to be learned by Loguserve sooner rather than later. If Loguserve found out on their own versus being told by Zazas, trust would be further damaged and negotiations would become that much more contentious and challenging.

Curiously, one of the more interesting conversations during the preparation phase of the process was around the two parties and their respective BATNAs. Beginning with Zazas, the reality was that if Loguserve did not agree to the new relationship, Zazas would have had to back down or shift to different terms. If they did not, and Loguserve walked away, Zazas might very well have gone out of business. But that did not mean Loguserve had all the power. While Loguserve had many other streams of business, it would have been very financially painful for them to exercise their BATNA and walk away from Zazas' business. The trick for Zasas was to persuade Loguserve not to engage in a game of chicken.

Vantage and Zazas then discussed the franchise model that lay at the heart of their business. Zazas wanted a model that would ensure they met their own financial objectives, but they also had to consider the interests of their many and varied franchisees. Vantage spent time canvassing the franchisees. While Zazas Corporate had a good understanding of franchisee interests, it was important to involve them and give them a voice in the negotiation process, and ensure a robust and granular understanding of their needs, concerns, and constraints. One key insight that emerged from this "voice of franchisee" exercise was a deeper understanding of how financially critical it was to avoid scheduling deliveries during peak times – when the presence of a delivery truck took up parking spaces, discouraged potential customers form stopping and entering stores, and led to significant lost revenue. This would be a major sticking point. Loguserve wanted maximum flexibility when it came to the delivery of supplies. However, franchisees expressed multiple frustrations with unload time, and driver courtesy and professionalism. Zazas and Vantage agreed these might be easier to resolve.

The focus then shifted to mapping the landscape of key players and stakeholders. This led Zazas and Vantage to do a more thorough analysis of Loguserve's business than had previously been done in their other negotiations. What Vantage and Zazas determined was that this arrangement was with one segment of Loguserve's business – other divisions providing different products and services had previously not been part of any deal. The Vantage team suggested that this was an opportunity. As one takes current business away, there may be an opportunity to develop new business with Zazas in the future. It was certainly something for them to consider and determine how much of a benefit it could bring to Loguserve.[2]

Together Vantage and Zazas representatives drilled down into Loguserve's overall business model, how they made money, how they separated profit and loss statements across different divisions, and what their growth models were into the future. As Zazas and Vantage did their analysis, they realized that other large retailers had already gone down the road of changing their business model in a similar manner to what Zazas wanted to do – or were considering the possibility of doing so. Zazas believed a persuasive argument to Loguserve was that this was going to be a trend in the entire industry, and that they could negotiate a new agreement that would help Loguserve adjust to, and then get in front of, this industry trend.

The above analysis led to a strategy that included the following positioning to Loguserve, "Help us through this transition and, if you do so willingly, we will do some things that will be valuable for you." These tradeoffs would come in the form of looking at different regions and what the right sequence and timing would be so the changes would be as painless for them as possible. This would also help Loguserve to grasp that being a fourth-party logistic supplier (i.e. an integrator that assembles the resources, capabilities, and technology of its own and other organizations to design, build, and run supply chain solutions) was going to be a much bigger part of their business going forward.

The Negotiation

Zazas and Vantage agreed that not only was the content and framing of the negotiation important, but so too was the process. In the past the two sides simply traded term sheets in a very impersonal manner. This time, the strategy was to get the parties together so they could share Zazas' view of the business and where they thought things were trending in the subsequent short, medium, and long term (10 years). They wanted the process and the explanation to be very transparent as well as to share a robust understanding of Zazas' interests. Then the plan was to invite Loguserve to do the same.

The general goal was to try to build a solid foundation of strategic understanding of each other's businesses as a starting point. Despite the tension and past dislike, both sides did view the relationship as a strategic partnership that was deeply interdependent.

The pillars of Vantage and Zazas' strategy can be summed up as follows:

- The process was set up to a large degree to be collaborative and to seek ways to expand the pie.
- The entire industry was trending in this new direction and, instead of being reactionary, Loguserve could get in front of it – and a new contract with Zazas could help Loguserve do so.
- Even though they were taking some business away from Loguserve, Zazas wanted to look collaboratively at various regions and which would be best to shift current business from. If Loguserve's performance was poor (or unprofitable for Loguserve) in a region, Zazas would suggest taking business from there and not from a region doing well, to minimize the impact on Loguserve. In some regions Loguserve had growth prospects and had more work than they could handle, so Zazas pulling back would not be a detriment.

Vantage and Zazas set out to persuade Loguserve through the use of objective criteria. They focused a lot of attention on what the market was doing and how it was forcing the retailer to make these changes.

The upfront work to create a collaborative joint problem-solving process was worth it and worked to a degree early on. Nevertheless, given the suggested changes and the reality that set in for Loguserve, the process did get more adversarial as it wore on. The negotiation never collapsed, but very likely would have if the initial collaborative approach did not set a different tone.

In the final stages of the negotiation, the process began to drag on. It was unclear what the delay was all about and people on the Zazas side began to worry the deal might be in jeopardy. The different leaders at Zazas fell into two schools of thought. The first was that Loguserve was not to be trusted and were going to pull the rug out from under Zazas at the last minute. The other school of thought was that Loguserve was perceiving Zazas to be acting in an adversarial manner. Loguserve was simply trying to figure out what their best course of action was given this new reality.

Due to all the delays and the rumors that began to swirl, the Zazas and Vantage team decided the best course of action was to propose getting the senior people on both sides together in a room, and work through the rest of the deal – with joint agreement at the outset not to leave until the deal was done. It seemed very clear to all sides that a no-deal solution would be catastrophic to Zazas and would be extremely harmful to Loguserve as well.

With everyone in the room there was a final appeal to the integrity and reputation of Loguserve, but also directly to the key executive who ran the division Zazas primarily worked with. The lead negotiator from Zazas highlighted the few billion dollars in business Loguserve stood to lose. This question was posed to the executive: "Do you want to be the executive under whose watch this all unraveled?"

In the end, Zazas did a lot of things to meet Loguserve's interests and Zazas got essentially everything they wanted – a new agreement, flat pricing, some improvements in service level, and 5% switch to a secondary supplier.

Lessons Learned

There are many fascinating lessons from this example. This case, in particular, highlights some counterintuitive notions that were found through diligent analysis, preparation, and in-depth consideration of the other's positions and interests.

Lesson 1: Process Matters

The process of how Zazas and Loguserve had negotiated in the past was a very big reason for the distrust. The trading of term sheets was impersonal and left many things of value poorly understood and addressed. A new, more collaborative approach, where the parties came together to work on the issues jointly, resulted in a change in behavior as well as a change in the terms.

The lesson here is to think as much about process as substance. Too often negotiators don't spend time contemplating the best way to go about negotiating a complex agreement. Process choices can have a significant impact on the negotiation itself and can help to rebuild trust where it may have been previously lacking.

Lesson 2: Focus on the Bigger Trends

The magnitude of the negotiation task in this example was grand. Zazas was asking for a lot and, initially, was rightly worried about how Loguserve would react. Vantage not only helped Zazas think through Loguserve's business model, their growth model, and what they might need in all of this, but they also helped frame a key element in the negotiation. In order to be asking for such dramatic changes, there had to be a way to justify their perspective. Zazas did so by couching their stance in bigger industry trends that were coming in the future. They also framed this as important for Loguserve to get out in front of this trend, instead of being reactionary. It certainly helped that another similar retailer had already gone down the road Zazas was asking for. In the end, it seems that Loguserve was at least partly persuaded by Zazas' projections about the trends.

Lesson 3: BATNA Analysis

Finally, this case presents a very curious BATNA analysis. Zazas had quite a poor BATNA. Had Loguserve refused to accede to Zazas' demands and walked away, they would have been left in a very precarious situation. Yet Zazas achieved all of their key objectives. How could this be? The key was that Zasas did not disempower themselves by focusing only on their own weak BATNA; they engaged in analysis that showed Loguserve had almost as much to lose as they did.

Did Loguserve fail to do their own BATNA analysis of the situation? Did Loguserve not recognize the impact their walking away would have on Zazas? Loguserve probably did look at the situation mostly from their own point of view and realized they too needed the business badly. Had Loguserve fully considered Zazas poor BATNA, they might have pushed back a bit more on the overall changes Zazas wanted to make.

Notes

1. The only part of the supplies not provided by Loguserve to Zazas was the fresh foods aspect of their business.
2. The fresh foods division within Loguserve was a separate division with its own profit and loss statement. This might be a benefit to Loguserve overall, but it might require escalating this to the CEO to take a big-picture view and not just the view from within the divisions.

5

How a Bad BATNA, but a Strong Relationship, Sidestepped a Lawsuit and Created a Mutual Gain Solution

Anonymous contribution

The challenge of dealing with power is one of the most perplexing dilemmas that negotiators face. While power differentials frequently exist in negotiation, they are rarely if ever absolute, despite what many may think. That is largely because power in negotiation is relational in nature. For example, in order for Negotiator A to have power over Negotiator B, it follows that Negotiator B has to value what Negotiator A has or what they can do to them in the process. And even if Negotiator A were to exercise said power over Negotiator B, there is another problem. The parties still have to implement what was agreed to. When people are forced to do things, they rarely do them to the best of their ability. Hence implementation and future negotiations are impacted by the exercise of power in numerous ways.

All that stated, there are also certain dynamics that transcend power in negotiation, the most critical of which is the strength of the relationship. If the parties to a negotiation have a strong bond, they are much less likely to exert power over the other, even if they possess that ability.

The following case presents an instance where a significant power discrepancy existed, but due to the strength of the relationship the more powerful party eschewed exercising their power and instead they worked together to find a solution that benefitted them both.

Background and the Negotiation Challenge

In 1995, Jim, Bill, and Tim started a company in a rented room with a fax machine. They did not even have a computer at the time! Their company, Contrexo, an Architecture, Engineer, and Construction management firm (AEC), grew from those very modest beginnings into a moderate-size business by 2001 with a value of approximately $20 million.

At that time, Contrexo was approached by a large publicly traded AEC firm called Mantosar, which wanted to acquire them. After some rather straightforward negotiations, Contrexo became a wholly owned subsidiary of Mantosar. The three principals who created Contrexo began working at Mantosar. As part of their contract with Mantosar, the three had a noncompete clause for a period of five years.

As the three men worked in conjunction with Mantosar they became increasingly frustrated with the overall business model and experienced a strong feeling of disenfranchisement. Furthermore, they could not see a way to grow Contrexo. The former owners and senior managers wanted to make a change, but were forced to wait until their noncompete agreements had expired. At that juncture, they decided to leave as individuals – one by one. The idea was to leave slowly and start a new company similar to Contrexo.

Jim was the first to leave the firm. The remaining senior leaders would come over one at a time and get restarted that way. Jim began reaching out to major clients to let them know that they were on their own again and the new company began to get new contracts. Shortly after Jim left, Bill followed. Bill's departure did not follow their original plan, but Bill had reached his limits with Mantosar.

Approximately one week later, Jim got a phone call from Mantosar's president, Peter, and CEO, Ramon. Peter and Ramon explained that they needed to speak with Jim immediately because they were considering bringing litigation against their new company. Jim, of course, agreed to meet.

A few days later Peter and Ramon came to Jim's new office space near Boston. Bill flew out from the Denver area for the meeting. When the parties sat down, Peter straightforwardly asked, "What are your intentions with the new company you are forming?" As Jim and Bill thought about their answer, Ramon added that when both Jim and Bill left Mantosar, they forced a significant material change of leadership that required public reporting because Mantosar was a publicly traded company. Immediately Mantosar would have to take the goodwill off their books as a write-off, which amounted to approximately $11 million in value. This would impact their stock price and they simply could not allow that to happen.

Peter and Ramon then explained that the only option they would have would be to sue Jim and Bill personally. They candidly admitted that they might not win the lawsuit, but it would tie up Jim, Bill, and the new company professionally for seven years. As a result, Jim and Bill's new business would likely fall apart.

Jim and Bill had worked well with Peter and Ramon for a number of years and they all liked each other personally. Peter and Ramon did offer Jim and Bill their jobs back at Mantosar with significant pay increases. Neither Jim nor Bill were interested in that opportunity. Was that the end of the negotiation? Their BATNA – the lawsuit – would be a disaster. So what to do now?

Preparing to Negotiate

Unlike many of the cases in this book, there was little or no time to prepare for this negotiation. Jim and Bill knew that a meeting was scheduled, but did not really have a clear sense of what was to be discussed. Clearly there was an urgency to the meeting, since Peter and Ramon called and planned to show up the next day.

When this is the scenario, the negotiators involved have to think quickly on their feet or try to find time to step away to plan. Jim believed that thinking quickly on their feet was the only way to go in this case. As he explained, "Had we stepped away to consider what to do, they might very well have left and proceeded with the lawsuit. Stepping away was not an option. We had to keep them in the room, and at the table, or things might really have fallen apart."[1]

One thing was clear to Jim. Even though he did not think it all through strategically, he knew his BATNA was not a good one. He understood that a potential lawsuit could stop his new business in its tracks with no real hope for success.

The Negotiation

When the negotiation began, Peter and Ramon did not sugarcoat their perspective on the situation. What was happening was unacceptable to them and they were considering a lawsuit to rectify the current course of action. They also made it clear to Jim and Bill that they had a flight home that afternoon, and if a deal was going to get done, it needed to happen then and there. Furthermore, they also explained that if there was a lawsuit, they would notify all the Fortune 100 companies that Contrexo had served in the past. This would cause these Fortune 100 companies to hold back any new business until the lawsuit was resolved. As was previously mentioned, that could take years.

Jim recalled the thoughts running through his mind at the time. In his words, "The first thing that popped into my head was that this could be really, really bad. There were thirteen new employees coming over in the very near term and forty to fifty employees coming on board in the future. Everything would very likely come to a screeching halt. It was a very scary proposition." That stated, Jim did not react negatively. In fact, he let his emotions run through, acknowledged them, and then quickly got into brainstorming mode. One of the keys to doing that was the strong relationship he had with Peter in particular. They had worked together for quite a while, had built a rapport that enabled frank conversations, and neither wanted to harm the other.

Jim indicated to Peter and Ramon that there were probably ways to work this out and that a lawsuit would not benefit any of them. Jim asked if they would be willing to go to lunch, roll up their collective sleeves, and work this through. Peter and Ramon agreed to give it a try.

After some time brainstorming around the issue, Jim eventually hit on a new idea. He asked Peter and Ramon if he and Bill could buy back Contrexo. It was a novel idea and one that had not come up before. In the end, it was the solution they needed, but it would be far from simple. Per usual, the devil was in the details.

One problem was that Jim and Bill did not have the $11 million in cash or capital to do the deal. On a piece of paper they mapped out a sale price and how Mantosar would have to take back a loan of significant value. Peter and Ramon would have to deal with a write down they could take and what Jim and Bill could manage in loans. They went back and forth and stayed late into the night trying to work something through that would meet their respective needs. Jim and Bill negotiated a loan of $6 million, along with reasonable interest rates they felt they could manage. They also mapped out a continued relationship between the two companies into the foreseeable future. That took future competition off the table and ensured a profitable arrangement for both going forward. This plan also enabled Jim and Bill to keep the agreements they had in place with other vendors.

This broke new ground for Mantosar. They had never let a wholly owned subsidiary be bought back. Curiously, from Mantosar's perspective, a lawsuit might have actually made more sense to pursue. With this deal they took a loss and had to take back loans, among other things. The only explanation Jim could surmise as to why they went down the road of a negotiated deal was the preexisting relationship he had with Peter and the impact of a lawsuit on Mantosar's stock price.

After the ink dried, Jim and Bill had one more challenge to negotiate. The thirteen people who had agreed to be part of the new Contrexo organization were going to have to be sold on the agreement and the proposed way forward. Initially, these people were quite upset with the deal; they asked Jim, "Why do we have to buy our own company back?" Jim and Bill weathered the storm from these employees and explained to them the downside of the lawsuit and how their business would never have gotten off the ground. Furthermore, they explained they could keep the company and all the contracts going forward. This would enable the most seamless transition possible. Eventually, the employees came on board and have all prospered quite well since.

Lessons Learned

There are innumerable lessons within this case. In a situation where a lawsuit looked immanent and was logical for one party, a negotiated agreement emerged from the ashes. Here is why.

Lesson 1: The Value of Relationships

First, the value of the relationship between Jim and Peter saved this situation from escalating out of control. Peter was Ramon's protégé as well and so the relationship between the three of them was particularly strong. That did not mean Peter and Ramon were pushovers. As Jim explained, "Peter and Ramon can definitely be hard negotiators. If it had not been me, I can imagine them walking in, saying we are suing you, and walking out."[2] The positive relationship also helped Jim to keep his emotions from derailing the process. Clearly the stakes were high, but Jim reminded himself of his ability to talk with Peter and Ramon and convinced them that they could come up with a deal that worked for all of them.

Lesson 2: Your Reaction Matters

Second, how you react to different moves in negotiation matters considerably. As Jim emphasized, his and Bill's reaction to the initial statement by Peter and Ramon was vitally important. Had they said, "Do what you have to do," the negotiation would have been over before it started, and a lawsuit would have been forthcoming. However, by stepping back and briefly going to the balcony (i.e. going to lunch) Jim and Bill were able to manage their reactions effectively, thereby shifting the conversation back to an interest-based approach.

Lesson 3: Power Exists, but Will They Use It?

Third, sometimes a power differential in negotiation does not always unfold in the way the parties expect. In this case, Mantosar had a lot of power and ability to control the process and yet they showed a lot more flexibility than a pure power analysis might suggest. This may partly be due to the reality that while a lawsuit would have hurt Contrexo much more, it would have also negatively impacted Mantosar's stock price. As such, perhaps the power differential was not as great as it initially appeared.

Notes

1. Interview with the author.
2. Interview with the author.

6

Let's Walk Away, but Before We Do, Would You Consider . . .

Based on an interview with Paul Neale

As the reader will have observed in some of the previous cases, the concept of BATNA is critically important to negotiation. Sometimes, however, negotiators prematurely settle on their BATNA and walk away before really exploring all of their other options. This is somewhat normal to do in the preparation phase of the negotiation process, but it is important to understand that BATNAs are not static; they change as a negotiation progresses and new insights come to light. It is therefore fundamental that negotiators understand the dynamic nature of BATNAs and reassess them from time to time before making a final decision.

Couple the above BATNA analysis with the problem of decision makers not speaking directly to each other. When that happens there are many opportunities for misunderstanding and miscommunication. Such was the case in this scenario, where, after the author consulted with this company, they decided to take another look at the situation before exercising their BATNA and walking away. The two primary negotiators also came to realize the importance of speaking directly with each other.

When they did come to the table and talk, they worked through a creative idea that still enabled them both to gain – albeit in an unorthodox fashion.

Background and the Negotiation Challenge

DOAR is a global consulting firm advising lawyers and major companies involved in complex legal disputes with high damage awards. DOAR recently added a new service to help lawyers find and retain expert witnesses for various types of litigation. DOAR helps to bring these experts on board and negotiates the terms of their arrangement with the law firms and corporations that require their expertise. In one sense, they are middlemen negotiating on behalf of the expert, but they also have to do so in a manner that brings them revenue.

In this case DOAR was negotiating with the law firm of Pine and Whitney. Some of the lawyers that DOAR negotiates with have a strong competitive edge and often see negotiation as a positional battle where they try to squeeze out whatever they can in the deal.

DOAR tries to keep their agreements as straightforward as possible. In virtually every case the contract they use is agreed to fairly readily by their counterparts. The sticking points have tended to be around their retainer, who is paying the bill in the end, the liability involved, and when payment will be made for the services rendered. Sometimes DOAR's negotiations are complicated by the fact that they are not negotiating with the primary decision makers, or they have to go through other representatives, such as an insurance agency.

In this scenario, the negotiation was focused on DOAR providing an expert witness to Pine and Whitney and the terms under which they would do so in a lawsuit alleging several billions of dollars of potential exposure. Typically, DOAR works with the same firms on a regular basis and is not too concerned about some of the nuances of the contract. However, in this particular instance, the limited liability clause became a sticking point. Pine and Whitney wanted DOAR to remove its limitation of liability clause from the agreement. Typically the law firms DOAR negotiates with are willing to allow DOAR to limit its liability to instances of gross negligence or willful misconduct.

As was previously mentioned, Pine and Whitney wanted DOAR to remove any limitation to its liability. Therefore, Steve, a senior lawyer at Pine and Whitney who is focused on intellectual property litigation, had his associate strike the entire limited liability clause from the agreement. One of DOAR's associates, Jeff, who was in charge of the relationship, asked Steve why this was so important to him. Steve explained that it is the law firm's policy never to sign an agreement with any kind of limited liability waiver included. The representatives of DOAR and Pine and Whitney were at a positional standoff – one side claiming they never sign liability waivers, the other side insisting that they do and have done so in the past. So, what to do now?

Preparing to Negotiate

Jeff came back to Paul, the CEO of DOAR, and explained where the negotiation stood. Pine and Whitney really wanted to work with the highly qualified expert DOAR had identified, but they simply wouldn't accept the limited liability waiver clause of the contract. As part of their internal conversation, Jeff and Paul discussed the size of the amount in dispute in the litigation and the remote possibility that something might lead to a liability claim. The two concluded that the chances were indeed very small, but they would be setting a precedent for the future that they were not comfortable with on a number of levels. However, they did know that this client was representing a major corporation in a multibillion-dollar case, so it would not take much of a liability claim to hobble DOAR if something did go wrong on the witness stand or during the deposition.

Paul's first response, if they would not sign some type of limited liability waiver, was that they wouldn't be able to work with them and he would have to exercise his BATNA and walk away from the deal. He had concluded that it was simply not worth the risk. However, before making a final decision they happened to have arranged a negotiation seminar led by the author and their thinking began to change. The author probed a little deeper into the situation, inquiring as to why the client did not want to sign the liability form. Jeff and Paul admitted that they were not really certain.

After the negotiation training, Paul spoke to Jeff and asked who they were working with at Pine and Whitney. Jeff said he was dealing with Amy, another associate at Pine and Whitney. Paul then asked, "Have you ever spoken to Steve, the senior partner, who has this issue and is the ultimate decision maker?"[1] Jeff confirmed that he had not spoken to Steve. Paul explained to Jeff that they needed to know what was really going on and why there was resistance on the part of Steve to signing the waiver. Paul shared with Jeff that DOAR had worked with other senior partners at Pine and Whitney and that they had never had this problem. They needed to get to the bottom of what was really going on.

The Negotiation

The following day Paul and Jeff got on the phone with Amy and Steve. After some compulsory small talk, Paul explained that he had worked with Pine and Whitney before, and with other senior partners, and there had never been a problem agreeing to the limited liability waiver clause. Paul asked Steve what was different this time. Steve explained that it had actually been the law firm's policy for a long time not to sign such waivers and he was quite unclear as to why other senior partners had signed the waivers previously. Steve went on to say rather abruptly, "If I am the only one who pays attention and does what the firm wants, that is the other guy's problem. This is a firm policy and I could not change it if I wanted to."[2]

Paul understood Steve's point and it was not the first time he had such a conversation with a senior partner in the industry. Paul acknowledged that he could appreciate the point and that there would be no hard feelings if they could not find a solution to this negotiation challenge. Paul then asked Steve to give him a little more time so he could think things through and make certain there was not another avenue to go down. Paul pledged to get back to him in the next few days.

After the call, Paul and Jeff began to brainstorm ideas. After some creative thinking they landed on the idea of having Pine and Whitney hire the expert directly, with DOAR getting out of the middleman role. Initially Paul and Jeff figured that they would lose out on the short-term revenue, but would preserve the longer-term relationship that was important to them. They also knew that this arrangement could only be done if DOAR agreed because the expert was under an exclusive contract with DOAR and Pine and Whitney was also on a contract with DOAR.

Before landing on this option definitively, they tried to take the idea a little further. Eventually Jeff called the expert, who very much wanted the job, and said, "You are billing DOAR at $500 per hour. We are billing the client at $800 so we make our profit. What if we have you work directly with the client and you pay us a $300 per hour referral fee. Then you and the client figure out the liability language and other sticking points directly without DOAR involved."[3] The expert was a professor and a one-person LLC, so the risk to him was much less. In return, DOAR offered to help the expert with the billing arrangement and a few other logistical matters. The expert agreed to do this with DOAR and to sign a side agreement delineating the terms.

Paul and Jeff then went back to Steve and explained that he was fine to work directly with the expert in this instance. Steve thanked them and ultimately worked out a deal directly with the expert in question.

In the past, Paul explained, they would have exercised their BATNA and simply walked away without really analyzing all the possibilities. Now, however, they have a different precedent for handling these more challenging negotiations in the future.

Lessons Learned

There are quite a few lessons embedded in this case and they are worth exploring in some detail. One, in particular, related to BATNA and resisting the urge to act too quickly is central to the story.

Lesson 1: Look behind the Position of "Sorry That Is Our Policy" to Underlying Interests

First, it is not uncommon to ask a negotiator if they are able to do something and to be met with the reply, "I am sorry, it is company policy." Such was the case here. What can you do as a negotiator if that is the response you receive? It is important to recognize that company policy is a position. The question is, what is the reason for the policy? What is the underlying interest behind the policy? While those questions were asked and did not yield a firm answer in this example, it did begin to get Paul and Jeff thinking about what else they could do to meet their interests.

Lesson 2: Negotiate with the Decision Maker Whenever Possible

Second, there are numerous challenges when you are not dealing with the ultimate decision maker. This case showed how assumptions, miscommunication, and misperceptions of intentions can all arise if decision makers are not talking directly to each other. This is particularly critical when a negotiator does not understand why a block is happening or what interests underlie a stated position.

Lesson 3: Thinking through BATNAs Carefully Yields Breakthroughs

Third, this example shows the power of thinking through one's BATNA carefully. After their analysis, Paul and Jeff realized that if they exercised their BATNA by removing themselves from one negotiation as go-between with the client and expert, they could meet their objectives by engaging in another negotiation, a different process separately with the client. They also creatively structured things so that they could still get paid for the work they had done of connecting the expert with the client, but taking the risk off the table for them. The risk to the expert in this situation was much less significant because he was a single-person LLC. As such, the expert wanted the work and had a different tolerance for risk that met the interests of all involved.

Lesson 4: An Outside Consultant Can Help with Perspective Taking

Finally, part of what triggered this new way of thinking and analysis was bringing in an outside consultant to help with the negotiation process. While the consultant was brought in generally, organizations should consider soliciting the assistance of someone from the outside to push their thinking and question their assumptions. This person can help "unhinge" people from their particular viewpoint – thereby making breakthroughs possible.

Notes

1. Interview with the author.
2. Interview with the author.
3. Interview with the author.

7

Walking the Negotiation Tightrope between Short-Term Needs and Developing Long-Term Relationships

Based on an interview with Seth Goodman

Anytime a new entity takes over a key relationship, there are sure to be many negotiations to follow. Some of those negotiations will be easier than others. For all those negotiations, however, the short-term needs must be balanced with cultivating the long-term relationships. If that happens the most beneficial arrangement will appear, but it is easier said than done.

This was the case in the example below, where a company took on the representation of a larger entity and had to negotiate a series of contracts with a subcontractor. In the end the parties reached a successful pact that benefitted them both, but it required a few risky moves and the sending of certain signals by the new representative to the other negotiator. While there was a lot of room for misinterpretation, the parties managed their way through these tests and reset the relationship to everyone's satisfaction.

Background and the Negotiation Challenge

Rambling Recyclers (RR) is a midsize national waste and recycling company based in the Southeast. RR has been growing steadily since it was formed and serves as a single point of contact for larger companies to manage all their waste needs. They do this through a unique networking model that has proven to be very effective.

Recently RR was awarded a national service contract with a very big food manufacturer, called Savory Grain Products (SGP). SGP is a family business that has existed for more than one hundred years – beginning on the West Coast but branching out across the country and becoming a household name. SGP needed an entity to manage all its waste, which is considerable, and entered into a five-year contract with RR for that purpose. RR was trying to get SGP to recycle more than they have in the past and to save them money in the process.

As RR began to get oriented to their new role, one of the contracts they had to manage was related to a company called AL Recovery (ALR). ALR's business is to take food waste from companies such as SGP, process the waste, and then turn the wasted food into animal feed for larger animals, such as cows and pigs. In this context, the waste means manufacturing food waste – such as wheat grains and rice – that fall to the floor as part of the food processing progression. By most estimates, about 8 to 10% of the food put into this process becomes waste. In bigger plants there are many millions of pounds of food put through this process each year, which results in a lot of waste – and a lot of opportunity.

ALR serviced eight of SGP's food processing plants in the aforementioned manner, which was approximately a third of SGP's plants. ALR had varying contracts for each of the eight plants they serviced. Some contracts were long term, others were short term or expiring, and at two of the plants, there were no contracts at all and services were provided on an ad hoc basis. RR needed to analyze these contracts, renegotiate them on behalf of SGP, and try to save SGP money in the process as RR had promised in their bid. This is where the negotiations came into the picture.

One of the heads of RR, named Bill Marks, undertook the renegotiations with ALR and their founder and CEO, Arnold Katz. Arnold, who is now in his early 90s, still maintained an active role in the company. Bill reached out to Arnold to find a time to talk. Bill agreed to fly to Texas to meet Arnold where he lives to make it most convenient for him.

Preparing to Negotiate

As Bill began to consider the negotiation, he knew that he needed to make a good impression on SPG early on. After all, he had just been awarded an important contract where he promised to save them at least 10% on the new contracts he was going to negotiate.

Bill began to conduct some background research on ALR and their business portfolio. As he did so he learned some interesting things about ALR. First, he learned that ALR had very varied contracts with each of SPG's plants, ranging from four years to no contracts at all. RR also knew that they were in a good position to negotiate because they had a strong BATNA. There were other suppliers who would jump at the chance to serve SPG and take over this business.

Bill and his team determined that their strategy needed to be to go to ALR with the following proposal. They would explain that they imagined that SRP was a good contract for them and that RR would like to sign ALR to new longer-term (four-year) contracts at each plant if they would tear up all existing contracts and agree to a decrease in their price to SRP.

RR and ALR had worked together before on some other projects so this was not a completely new relationship. RR reached out to ALR and let them know they had won the business to represent SRP and asked that they share all relevant documents with RR as SPG's official recycler. ALR complied with that request. The regional manager contacted Bill and explained that for a deal of this magnitude he would have to speak to the company's owner and CEO, Arnold. Bill had heard about Arnold's reputation. He was a nonagenarian and known for being a somewhat tough micromanager. He was also worth several hundred million dollars.

Bill tried to think about what would be important to a nonagenarian beyond the money. Clearly his end of life was in sight – so what would he really want? Since he was still the dominant player in his business, he must enjoy what he does. Bill also reminded himself that RR wanted to win big contracts in the future and ALR could be a great long-term partner on many of these contracts. There was a short-term negotiation to engage in, but also a long-term relationship that could bear considerable fruit. Bill knew he had to try to thread the needle between the two.

The Negotiation

Arnold invited Bill out to lunch where he lives in Texas. Bill was happy to go with a colleague and be deferential to Arnold. As Bill explained, "Arnold was very well dressed, presented very well, and was a really nice guy."[1] Bill was pleasantly surprised because he had created a contrary image in his mind of what Arnold might be like. That stated, Bill knew Arnold was very successful and a shrewd businessman, so he approached the situation with caution. The two men shared stories about their companies and Arnold talked at length about being a self-made millionaire and came across as wanting to impart wisdom on Bill and his colleague since they were considerably younger. Arnold praised Bill and RR for the idea behind their business and the value of being a one-stop recycling shop for SPG.

After a while they got down to the real reason they were meeting – to see if they could negotiate a new arrangement. Bill explained his offer in general. He shared that he felt RR and ALR could work together on this. In exchange for ALR doing away with their current contracts with SPG and paying a bit more, ALR would get a long-term contract with stability – something Bill surmised Arnold would want. Bill explained further that some contracts ALR had with SPG were competitive, while others were not, and they needed to rectify that issue. Bill sought to put a mutual gain frame on the negotiation. Bill also mentioned that if their negotiation went well ALR could be in line for more business with SPG. Arnold expressed interest in all of these possibilities and they left that phase of the negotiation with Bill agreeing to follow up and send Arnold a detailed offer for the contracts.

Bill recalled feeling very good after the meeting because he and Arnold had connected so well. In addition to this burgeoning relationship it also seemed that Arnold wanted to impart the valuable lessons he had learned to Bill and his colleague.

When Bill got back to his office, he and his team put together what he described as an aggressive offer — where in every site he was managing he put in a competitive ask for all the commodities he was buying. This first offer was, as Bill shared, "on the very high end of reasonable." In exchange, as promised, Arnold would get a long-term deal on the eight plants he was overseeing.

The following day this reply came from Arnold: "You are crazy and your prices are off the charts. Forget it. We will just wait it out and see what happens."[2] In part Arnold must have done his analysis and determined that Bill and RR had to show SPG savings and had that pressure on them. As Bill shared in retrospect, "We may have come across as too aggressive. Arnold could not make his margins based on what we were asking."[3] After this exchange, Bill felt that he had lost some leverage. Arnold was clear that he would stay with his current contracts, and if they were to expire, he would make bids for new ones.

At this juncture, Bill went back to the drawing board. He immediately started thinking about the two SPG facilities where ALR did not have contracts. Bill asked his team for options on those. In short order, his team found an option: a competitor who wanted to pick up one of the sites. It turned out that the site in question was right in Arnold's backyard. Before doing the deal, Bill reached out Arnold and gave him the courtesy of matching the offer. Arnold explained that he understood and that he would not counteroffer. They both wished each other luck and Bill reiterated his desire to work with ALR on the other sites.

Bill's deal with the other company seemed to persuade Arnold that Bill knew what he was doing and was not a pushover. This move sent a signal to Arnold that they were serious about these changes. Shortly thereafter Arnold came back to the table and said, "If you make me a reasonable offer, I am open, but your first offer was ridiculous."[4] Bill said he would consider a revision and get back to him shortly.

Using his initial offer, Bill came down enough to ensure he would get the 10% reduction he promised to SPG and gave ALR the four-year contract on all remaining sites. It was still a good deal for Bill and it kept the door open with Arnold and ALR for more partnering in the future.

One of the dynamics that really helped RR was that they had promised SPG a 10% reduction overall and not on each specific site. This created the flexibility they needed to piece different deals together to get to the 10% overall. As Bill explained, "This gave me a lot of room to move the chess pieces around on the chess board."[5]

In the end, Arnold accepted Bill's offer and Bill and Arnold developed a strong relationship with some long-term opportunities increasingly plausible. In fact, one option that has begun to emerge is the possibility of RR acquiring ALR. Either way, ALR has a lot of clients that RR would also like to have, and they are on a mutually beneficial trajectory together.

Lessons Learned

This case offers some very distinct insights given the nature of the relationship that RR had as an agent for a much larger entity and their need to rework a sensitive, and important, relationship with ALR without destroying it.

Lesson 1: First Offers

The first lesson has to do with first offers. In this example, Bill almost destroyed the prospect of a deal with a very aggressive first offer. While it is certainly acceptable to have an aspirational offer in mind it is critical that it does not cross a line into the unrealistic realm. If it does, as was witnessed herein, it can come across as an insult and shut down negotiations before they get started. In this instance Bill was fortunate that Arnold needed this deal and found his way back to the table.

Related to this was that the first offer also served as an anchor for the negotiation. When Arnold came back to the table Bill could have asked for a counteroffer. Instead, he worked off his initial proposal and came down from it in a manner that showed Arnold good faith, while still meeting his objectives.

This enabled Bill to keep control of the process. Had Bill done the opposite, and asked Arnold for a counteroffer, the gap in the Zone of Possible Agreement (ZOPA) might have been too large to bridge.

Lesson 2: Sending Signals in Different Ways

The second lesson is that there are many ways to send signals in negotiation and sometimes negotiators have to take a stand to show the seriousness with which they take the process and that they know what they are doing. In this example, Bill took a big risk by shifting one of ALR's sites to a competitor. This could have backfired and caused the process to break down all together. However, it had the opposite effect of showing Arnold that Bill remained true to his words and his actions.

Sending a signal such as this has to be done after stepping back and determining the overall negotiation landscape. In this situation Bill knew that the eight sites that ALR controlled were an important part of their business and they could not risk losing them all. Bill also knew he had a very good BATNA -- other competitors that would happily take ALR's contracts away from them. With those things in mind, Bill had a pretty good sense Arnold would come back around.

Lesson 3: Keeping the Door Open: Balancing the Short- and Long-Term

At various points in the process Bill was very careful to explain to Arnold that the door was still open to him coming back to the table. Bill clearly grasped the reality that a short-term deal related to SPG was important, but so was a potential long-term partnership (or acquisition) with ALR.

Had Bill simply gone about the negotiation with a short-term lens and not been clear that the long term was also important, Arnold might have felt disrespected and walked away.

Lesson 4: Likability Factor

In his seminal book *Influence*, Robert Cialdini discusses six means of persuasion.[6] One of the six is what Cialdini calls the likability factor, which is how much someone likes you and can relate to you. The likability factor played an important role in this negotiation. From the start of their interactions, Bill and Arnold personally connected. Arnold seemed to see a younger version of himself in Bill. Further, Bill and Arnold shared an ethnic heritage that led Arnold to want to impart lessons from his experience.[7]

It is always difficult to determine exactly how much the likability factor plays a role, but it is one of those things you notice when it exists. In this instance, both Bill and Arnold reported that there was a connection that helped them understand each other and want to do business together.

Lesson 5: Persistence and Not Overreacting

The last lesson from this case is the importance of persistence and not overreacting in negotiation. When Bill made his initial offer, and Arnold's terse reply came back steeped in frustration, some would have determined the negotiation – and for that matter the relationship – was over. Further, when the first plant was siphoned off by Bill and given to a competitor, one could have also concluded that was the end. However, with a big-picture view, Bill persisted and did not overreact. He sensed, based on other factors and a thorough analysis, that Arnold would come back, and he held the door open for him to do so.

Many people believe negotiations are over after they have gone down a road and hit a dead end. However, the best negotiators realize that will happen and look for other avenues to take a process down. That is when deals get saved from premature closure.

Notes

1. Interview with the author.
2. Email correspondence from Katz to Marks.
3. Interview with the author.
4. Email correspondence from Katz to Marks.
5. Interview with the author.
6. Cialdini, R. *Influence: The Psychology of Persuasion*, revised ed. (Pearson Books, 2008).
7. In Cialdini's book *Influence*, he lists six means of persuasion. In his more recent book, *Pre-suasion*, he lists a seventh, which is Unity, by which he means some connection based on identity, which is what Bill and Arnold shared. For more information, see R. Cialdini, *Pre-Suasion: A Revolutionary Way to Influence and Persuade* (Simon & Schuster, 2018).

8

Out from behind the Shadows

Contributed by Joshua N. Weiss

Many negotiations are genuinely not what they seem to be at the outset of the process. This is particularly the case when there are hidden parties, or influencers, that are operating behind the scenes and are the reason the negotiation is getting stalled. When this happens, it is hard to determine initially that this is the problem because those parties are in the shadows with one party not even knowing they are part of the equation.

Often these behind-the-scenes parties reveal themselves after some time, particularly when a key moment occurs in the negotiation process and their input is needed. That was the situation in the example below, when a shadow party was revealed only after a stalemate that put the process on the verge of collapse.

Background and the Negotiation Challenge

Engineering Experts Inc. (EEI) is an engineering consulting firm that works all over the world on large projects, including water management, transportation, and energy and facilities. They have multiple divisions that address every aspect of the engineering process from design to build and construction to program management. EEI works with many varied entities, including federal and state governments as well as industrial clients.

In this example, EEI was working with a city in the southwestern part of the United States called Amity County (AC). AC was desirous of designing and building a physical-chemical treatment plant for wastewater and EEI was serving as a consultant in both the design and build phases of the project.

EEI's project manager on the job was Stan. Stan had been with EEI for over 15 years, with another 5 years at another firm. AC's project manager was Alphonso. Alphonso was relatively new to the business, just two years out of college with his engineering degree from a middle-tier university in the southeast part of the country.

The project began well, with both Stan and Alphonso on the same page. Things stayed that way for a while until they ran into a problem with a system that EEI had proposed to install because the wastewater was too strong at the site. This was a bit of a surprise to Stan based on the data that he had seen. That stated, Stan quickly realized what was happening and reassured Alphonso that he knew how to fix the issue. Stan laid out his plan to do just that, but Alphonso met his ideas at every turn with a series of no's, which he delivered with very little explanation as to why he was rejecting Stan's new approach. If there was going to be a negotiation, Stan thought to himself, he would need to figure out what was going on and why Alphonso not only kept saying no, but what logic underlay his perspective.

Preparing to Negotiate

Stan wracked his brain but simply could not come up with a reason as to why Alphonso was rejecting his idea. Afterall, Stan was the expert with 20 years of experience. Alphonso was still green around the ears – only a few years out of college. But that was not what troubled Stan. What he could not get his head around was why.

In his desperation, Stan reached out to a colleague, Amy, who had done considerable training in the field of negotiation and conflict resolution. As Stan began to describe the scenario to Amy, she quickly realized that there was an underlying interest that Alphonso had that was hidden. If Stan was going to solve this negotiation problem, he needed to get Alphonso to share this information. Part of the problem was that Stan was not the best communicator, so he preferred to rely on email for most of his interactions. In fact, Stan and Alphonso had only met once in person since the project initiation meeting three months earlier. Amy emphasized the importance of building the relationship with Alphonso as one critical way in which Stan could get him to talk and share what was really going on. Stan reluctantly agreed and reached out to Alphonso, asking him to have lunch. Alphonso agreed and the two planned to meet a few days later.

From Alphonso's perspective, he was in a real quandary. He was in over his head and did not have the experience to really know what to do, or if what Stan was suggesting was the right course of action. Alphonso did not feel like he could go to his boss, who had been skeptical of hiring someone so young in the first place. Alphonso was relying on Stan to guide him – that is why AC hired EEI in the first place – but he was nervous. He needed to get this right to show his boss he could manage it. Now this issue had arisen with Stan and the project timeline and budget were thrown into question. Why didn't Stan know about the strength of the water? If he was really good at what he did, he would have known this (at least that is what Alphonso thought to himself).

When this problem emerged, Alphonso did the only thing he could think of. He reached out to Ralph, a family friend, who had inspired him to get into the engineering field in the first place. Ralph, who had been retired for five years, was a kind and gentle soul who had offered to mentor Alphonso if he needed it. At first Alphonso hesitated to reach out to Ralph for fear of looking incompetent. However, he realized it was better to look that way to Ralph than to Stan and certainly to his boss!

When Alphonso and Ralph finally talked, Ralph did nothing to assuage Alphonso's fears. In fact, he stoked them. He explained that Stan probably should have picked this up right away and there was only one way to address the problem. Ralph shared that idea with Alphonso and emphasized that if Stan suggested other efforts he should hold firm to Ralph's suggestion. He had seen this approach work in the past and knew it was viable. Alphonso confirmed that he understood the essence of what Ralph was sharing and would explain this Stan. This is the point at which the overt negotiation commenced.

The Negotiation

After a number of emails back and forth between Alphonso and Stan prior to the lunch, where Alphonso kept pushing for Ralph's suggested approach, and Stan kept trying to explain why that was not the best way forward, Stan kept emphasizing the importance of meeting in person. Even though they had agreed to meet for lunch, Alphonso was getting cold feet. Alphonso had a negotiation style that can best be described as avoidance. He felt very uneasy with difficult personal interactions and was sensing this negotiation with Stan would very likely fit that mold. Alphonso simply felt safer using email. Stan kept insisting on meeting in person and Alphonso finally relented and agreed to have lunch. Meanwhile close to a week had transpired and if they did not act soon the timeline would begin to slip.

When the two of them finally got together, Stan began by explaining that he knew how to fix the problem and could not understand why Alphonso was not taking his advice. He emphasized that was why AC had hired Stan and EEI. Alphonso stonewalled for a while, not wanting to tell Stan about Ralph. He was feeling the pressure from Stan and his anxiety eventually overcame him. Alphonso abruptly ended the meeting by walking out. Stan was even more confused now than before.

Perplexed, Stan went back to the office and called Amy immediately. His face was red and he was, simply put, ready to explode. He tried to settle himself down, but it took a while. Finally, he got to a point where he could recount what had happened. Amy listened carefully and emphasized that these processes can take time and he needed to try again with Alphonso. She also explained the notion of avoidance and how that was likely part of the equation. Amy again reiterated that Stan needed to find a way to make Alphonso comfortable so he could share what was really going on for him. It was the only way to solve the problem.

Stan sent Alphonso an email later that day explaining that he felt badly that Alphonso had become quite anxious and wanted to try to meet again. He asked two things: that Alphonso pick the place and that he come and just listen to Stan's proposed plan. If, after hearing him out, he still did not want to go down that road, Stan would consult with his boss. The next morning Alphonso replied and agreed – reluctantly.

Two days later Stan and Alphonso met at a small restaurant across from Alphonso's office. When Stan arrived, he saw Alphonso standing with an elderly gentleman. Alphonso had asked Ralph to come to the meeting to hear from Stan for himself and to help Alphonso understand things in more detail. Alphonso introduced Stan to Ralph and explained Ralph's background. Alphonso then shared that Ralph had been giving him advice on what to do on this project in general and with this issue in particular. As the three of them sat down together, Stan was beginning to put the pieces together of what had been going on.

Stan started from the beginning and shared with both men why he did not initially see the issue with the water. Then he respectfully asked Ralph how long he had been retired. Ralph explained that it had been five years. Stan went on to share that a new approach to dealing with this kind of problem had been used the last few years – with great success. Ralph admittedly had not heard of this new approach given that he had largely stepped away from the engineering world and confessed that he was "not up on the latest approaches." As Stan proceeded to share the nuances of the approach, Ralph grasped what Stan was explaining. It turns out, so did Alphonso to a large degree because he had let go of being defensive and was finally listening to Stan. By the time the three of them had finished lunch, Alphonso was on board with Stan's plan and confident that he would be able to implement it. There was one more problem, however.

Alphonso was still not clear on how to explain this shift to his boss and worried that if his boss started asking him all kinds of detailed questions, he would not have the knowledge to respond. While the shift would not cost any additional resources, there was the need to share how this new approach would solve the problem. When Alphonso raised the concern with Stan, an easy fix came to Stan's mind. Stan offered to walk this all through very carefully with Alphonso again and then also told him he would be happy to accompany him to meet with his boss. If there was anything Alphonso was struggling to explain, Stan would jump in and provide some additional insights. Alphonso was relieved at this approach and Stan was more than happy to oblige so that he could finally get on with fixing the problem. With all the delays they were behind schedule, but they could get back on track in the near future once this was signed off.

Lessons Learned

There are a few fundamental lessons within this case – many of which lay underneath the surface. For this negotiation to reach a successful conclusion, these issues needed to be brought to the forefront to truly understand what was happening.

Lesson 1: Uncovering Hidden Interests

This negotiation is a classic case of the importance of uncovering hidden interests that are getting in the way of a viable solution. In this example, Alphonso was relatively new and did not want to appear to his boss like he did not know how to do his job. He needed to save face and, due to his lack of comfort communicating, was unsure how to do that.

Stan had the good sense to understand there was something going on under the surface that he did not understand. Consulting his colleague Amy helped to reinforce this and to keep his mind focused on figuring out what he did not know. When he eventually uncovered the real reason for the stalemate, he could deal with it effectively. Sometimes playing the role of inspector or investigative journalist is necessary in negotiation.

Lesson 2: Mapping the Parties and Understanding All the Influencers Can Be Key to Success

Sometimes the parties to a negotiation are very clear. However, it is still important to map the primary parties and, very importantly, the secondary parties who are not actually sitting at the main table, but have a considerable impact on the outcome. It is quite common for negotiators to have to consider those metaphorically sitting behind the other negotiator and what is important to them.

In this particular example, Ralph's presence and input was the key to solving this negotiation conundrum. That stated, it would have been hard for Stan to determine this at the outset of the negotiation. As the process wore on, however, it would have been good if he was thinking that it might be possible there was someone behind Alphonso who was influencing him. Had he considered that possibility, he might have explored that a bit further with Alphonso and come to understand what was really going on sooner.

Lesson 3: The Medium Matters

The medium through which you negotiate always has pros and cons. Negotiation in person can be very effective for reading body language and nonverbal clues, but it can also be an anxiety-producing experience.

Similarly, negotiating via email, as was done in this case, can sometimes block progress. This is particularly the case when people don't read between the lines and don't explore underlying interests and what is meant by certain statements. Stan and Alphonso's email interactions were very positional in nature with very superficial back-and-forth interactions. In order to use email effectively in negotiation, the parties have to probe for underlying interests and ask clarifying questions when the other negotiator makes potentially perplexing statements. If negotiators do these few things their interactions will greatly improve, and email will not be something to be avoided, but to be used carefully and thoughtfully.

II

International Business Cases

With the interconnected nature of the world, more and more companies are working internationally. As a result, an increasing number of negotiations are taking place across borders and between businesses stretching from Afghanistan to Zimbabwe. Business deals are happening everywhere, in some of the most unlikely places, and between some of the most unlikely partners.

Negotiation in this context has a number of added dimensions that negotiations in the domestic context need not consider. Just two examples will suffice. First, laws differ from country to country and it is often unclear which laws will be applicable in a given situation. Second, unique cultural norms undergird each negotiator's overall orientation. Unless those cultural differences are understood deeply, they can easily disrupt a process that otherwise would flow smoothly.

This section will cover a number of distinct cases that occur entirely within other countries (i.e. outside the United States) or between businesses from one country to another. The challenges are significant, as you will come to see, and rife with potential areas of trouble.

The first case has to do with a very interesting scenario of a company, called Innoagri, that needed to buy a certain piece of equipment in China from a company called Solantar.

The problem Innoagri faced was that Solantar was the only one that produced this equipment in the *entire* country. When Innoagri approached Solantar about the purchase, Solantar explained that they could supply them with the equipment, but they were dramatically increasing their price. What was Innoagri to do in the face of such a challenge and with nowhere to turn? You will be surprised by what transpired.

The second case typifies what happens when a negotiation between very powerful players gets addressed in the public eye. Two wealthy businessmen, Abilio Diniz and Jean-Charles Naouri, became locked in a high-profile negotiation that had escalated out of control. Many millions of dollars were being expended on lawyers and other assistance in an effort to "win" the negotiation. The dynamic only changed when a negotiation consultant began assisting Diniz and Naouri – helping them get down to the underlying issues that were driving their behavior and at the core of what they needed. Once those human needs were articulated by both sides, a simple way out emerged that broke the cycle and allowed both Diniz and Naouri to get on with the life they wanted to lead.

The third case occurred in the Middle East with a company involved in aluminum production, called Iron Works, and a shipping company, called Seabourn Trading, charged with delivering the raw materials for production. The negotiation transpired within the context of a long history of working together, but with some previously unknown information that Iron Works discovered about Seabourn Trading. As that new information came to light a revised relationship was forged, albeit not without significant hurdles and roadblocks the negotiators had to manage in order to reach a deal acceptable to both.

The fourth example transpired between two large companies, PPM and Arma, and was related to Arma's acquisition of PPM's business. Arma was based in the United States and PPM, who was selling part of their company, was based in a country in Europe. The initial negotiation seemed to go fairly smoothly, until the eleventh hour, when PPM pulled a key facility from the deal. Fearing the loss of all the progress made to date, Arma and PPM still consummated the deal, but also put in place a poorly thought through manufacturing supply arrangement to supplant the business that would have transitioned had the aforementioned facility been part of the deal. Almost immediately after the signing of the agreement, the supply arrangement started breaking down. After trying to work through the situation on their own, Arma sought the services of a negotiation consulting firm, which ultimately helped the parties address the underlying issues and find a better way forward.

The fifth example occurred during a significant political shift in Europe. As the landscape was changing radically in the early 1990s, due to the collapse of the former Soviet Union and its impact on Europe, two negotiators representing a German-based company called Agency in Trust and a French-based company called CGE (later Vivendi) found themselves at the heart of a negotiation that went to the identity of the countries involved. By understanding the bigger picture and thinking creatively about how to bridge the obvious gaps in the parties' respective positions, the negotiators were able to overcome a significant impasse and meet their respective interests.

The sixth example is a classic challenge related to power and why wielding power carefully is so very important. A fledging US-based startup, run by Steve, had run into cash flow problems. Without an infusion of money they would go under. A French partner, run by Pierre, emerged that was willing to provide Steve and the startup with the infusion of capital they needed. The French company came to understand during the negotiation that they had a very strong upper hand and Pierre decided to exploit it for their maximum benefit. Of course, that left a bad taste in the mouth of Steve and his startup, who felt exploited in the negotiation. There was little that Steve could do in the situation so he had to accept it. However, a few years later Pierre and his French company sought to go public. As a result, they had to shed their ownership in the startup, which was no longer struggling and in a much better financial position. That negotiation did not end well for Pierre due to how he had wielded power in the initial negotiation.

The seventh illustration of a difficult negotiation that found a mutually acceptable solution was based in a country in Europe. The negotiation surrounded the handing over of a family business between a father, named Marcel, and his son, Louis. It is fair to say that they had a strained relationship at best. Other familial dynamics, rooted in a long history of both love and frustration, stood in the way of Marcel's dream and Louis's reality. With the help of a consultant the parties were able to find a way ahead, but this required healing old wounds along the way.

The eighth case study in this section has to do with a negotiation centered around the development of a certain specialized technology for a product. A company in Canada, called CXX Technology, was developing a laser to project a virtual keyboard onto any surface. The manufacturing was very difficult to achieve despite their many efforts to get it developed. Ultimately, due to funding and technical expertise, the company in Canada decided to use a company in China, called Manufix, for such a task. Despite having done their due diligence, as the project unfolded it became clear to CXX Technology that Manufix lacked the ability to actually do part of the work required. Because they were significantly far along in the project, changing course would be very costly and would badly disrupt CXX Technology's timeframe to go to market. Instead of walking away, CXX Technology found a way forward that met their objective through addition, not subtraction.

The ninth case in this section had to do with the importance of relationship building as a core component to a relatively new engagement between the parties. The smaller of the two companies, called Ecru, very much desired the opportunity to work with the larger entity in India, called Indegopro. Faced with a real power discrepancy, the negotiator representing Ecru traveled halfway around the world to build the relationship with Indegopro and seal the deal. The simple act of showing up – albeit not simple in practice due to the time and effort involved – was the key to getting Indegopro to say yes.

The last case, the tenth in the section, is a classic example of a cross-cultural negotiation that ran into numerous problems and issues due to a lack of understanding by one side. A South Korean company, called Kyammi, was trying hard to work with the other company, a German entity called Bundascorp, in what they believed to be a culturally appropriate manner. Unfortunately, the representative of Bundascorp was not conscious of the cultural differences that lay at the heart of the negotiation between them. As such, the parties were able to reach an agreement, but the Kyammi representative concluded the negotiation feeling very dubious about the outcome and the future relationship.

9

Negotiating Effectively in the Face of a Significant Power Imbalance

Based on an interview with Raphael Lapin

There are times when negotiation success in a given context seems almost impossible. The three words that often invoke such a perspective are *sole supplier negotiation*. When someone has to negotiate with a sole supplier, which means that a supplier has a monopoly on an item or service, they usually have very little leverage to do so. They are typically confronted with a binary decision – to buy on the supplier's terms or not to buy at all. There is often not much choice for the unfortunate buyer, and the stage is typically set for exploitation.

In this case example, the reader will see that negotiations of this type are not always what they seem. Good preparation, constructive questioning of key assumptions, and really creative thinking can alter the balance of power in this kind of negotiation, enabling the parties to reach an agreement. Here is how it was done.

Background and the Negotiation Challenge

The buyer in these negotiations, called Innoagri, was a manufacturer of heavy agricultural implements and mining equipment in Shanghai. In addition to their Chinese clients, Innoagri also exported to clients internationally. Innoagri's current operations were working on outdated machinery, and they needed to purchase new machinery to streamline their processes, and improve their operations and products in order to keep up with their formidable competition, both locally and abroad. The problem was that the supplier of this much-needed machinery, Solantar, was the only source for this equipment in *all* of China. Solantar was protected by the government in order to maintain control over this important aspect of the manufacturing industry. As an aside, in China it is common for a supplier to have a monopoly on a particular industry. In fact, in some cases a monopoly may be protected by the government due to personal relationships, or other political or financial interests. In other cases, the government may even have significant equity ownership in the company.

In addition to the capital purchase, Innoagri also desired a service contract for the machinery. Solantar was demanding an exorbitant price for both the capital equipment and the service contract. Importing the equipment from another country would be prohibitive for Innoagri due to the severe protectionist government regulations in place.

A negotiation consultant was retained by Innoagri and tasked with helping its procurement team prepare for the negotiation with the objective of reaching an agreement on a more reasonable price. This was a tough task indeed.

Preparing to Negotiate

The procurement team from Innoagri was comprised of three Chinese nationals and two Australians. After some carefully targeted questions and further information transfer, the consultant began to understand the severity of the situation. This consultant had to think very carefully and creatively to find some potential path forward to resolve the dilemma. The consultant, after secluding himself for some time, came up with an idea that might help to guide the procurement team in this seemingly untenable negotiation. The consultant challenged the negotiating team to rigorously consider what they might do if Solantar suddenly went out of business. To make the challenge even harder, the consultant insisted on a three-day deadline for a solution to this hypothetical problem.

At first the team from Innoagri was stunned and thought the task they had been handed was impossible. However, after some self-pity, they broke out of that way of thinking and began to brainstorm and explore all sorts of possibilities. One idea that emerged was to try to reengineer their own design, thereby obviating the need for this machinery altogether. Another idea was to talk to a company that manufactured similar equipment and to discuss the possibility of retooling that equipment to meet Innoagri's needs. While creative, neither idea seemed very workable in practice.

Eventually, one of Innoagri's procurement team members came up with a third idea. He suggested researching other customers of the supplier who might have bought this machinery in the past and be willing to sell it now. After some further contemplation and several phone calls, the team found a customer in Mongolia who was willing to sell their used but still working equipment to Innoagri. Having no further current need for the equipment, the company in Mongolia was happy to discuss selling it and trying to recoup part of their investment. This was the breakthrough Innoagri had hoped for. Although their first choice was still to purchase new equipment with warranties and service agreements from Solantar, this was a viable BATNA that they could live with, should it be necessary.

The Negotiation

Equipped with this improved BATNA, the mood in Innoagri shifted dramatically from despair to optimism and from an imbalance of power to more of a level playing field. Put differently, Innoagri was now equipped with the needed leverage to achieve a reasonable price from Solantar. The Innoagri team presented their proposal to Solantar, with a figure slightly better than their reservation point, and significantly below the initial inflated price that Solantar had demanded. The Innoagri team indicated to Solantar that they wanted to do business with them, but at the same time, made it clear to them that they did have a credible alternative should negotiations fail.[1]

As the negotiations progressed, Innoagri's representatives were actually able to start a bidding war between Solantar and the Mongolian entity who wanted to sell their used equipment. After intense and somewhat lengthy negotiations, Innoagri got a very reasonable deal for themselves and something Solantar could also live with in terms of the equipment sales and the service contract. That evening, both the negotiation consultant and the Innoagri team enjoyed celebratory cold beers like never before.

Lessons Learned

Negotiating with a sole supplier can be one of the most challenging situations for a business. As the reader has been able to comprehend from this example, despite the belief that there is very little that can be done in these situations, with some creative thinking and hard work the negotiation landscape can be changed. The lessons below highlight the best chance for success when confronted with this type of scenario.

Lesson 1: Be Prepared

First, this negotiation is an excellent example of why preparation is so critical. Preparation provides you with the confidence and composure to stay on course toward your objectives and not give away more than is necessary. Innoagri worked very hard to find a better BATNA, and it was all due to their preparation. In addition to improving their BATNA, the preparation that was done here also helped to preempt any potential surprises that may have presented themselves during the negotiation. While all of these things cannot be anticipated in every negotiation, many of them can be through this careful analysis.

Lesson 2: Thinking through Your BATNA Carefully

Second, the critical factor to this negotiation was Innoagri rigorously exploring their alternatives and BATNA. Although initially it appeared that Innoagri had no leverage at all and a very poor BATNA, with the help of their consultant Innoagri was able to improve their BATNA dramatically. With this new BATNA Innoagri felt much more confident and negotiated in that manner with Solantar. Solantar was forced to adjust their negotiation position when they realized that Innoagri did indeed have a viable alternative.

Lesson 3: Assumptions Wreak Havoc on Negotiation

Third, it is essential for a negotiator to closely examine all the assumptions they make in a given negotiation. Innoagri initially assumed that they were dealing with a sole source supplier and, more importantly, they had no other way forward. By carefully challenging that belief, and being prepared to abandon this assumption, their minds were free to unlock other creative possibilities.

Lesson 4: Outside Eyes Can Be Very Valuable

Finally, when preparing for a negotiation, enlist the help of a consultant or a person within your organization who has some background in negotiation, but who is not directly involved in the specific negotiation in question. A fresh and informed perspective will challenge assumptions and can help to induce more expansive and creative thinking among the negotiators and how they approach the challenge.

Note

1. Introducing a BATNA to one's counterpart always brings with it a certain degree of risk, because they may perceive it as a threat, which will make them defensive. This required careful coaching as to how to introduce the BATNA in a way that was credible and at the same time mitigated these risks.

10

Breaking a Negotiation Deadlock through Intangibles[1]

Based on an interview with William Ury

Deadlocks are nothing new in negotiation. However, when parties take a positional approach to negotiation, with very high stakes involved and with much of the negotiation playing out in the public sphere, the stage is set for a perfect storm of confounding and self-defeating behavior. When this confluence of events comes together in just the right way, otherwise attainable objectives remain elusive.

This was indeed the case when my colleague William Ury heard from the daughter of one of the people embroiled in this negotiation quagmire. She implored Ury to get in touch with her father to try to help him out of this seemingly endless trap. Ury agreed, but with some trepidation, wondering what he could offer. After meeting with the father and asking some critical questions, Ury could begin to see a possible way through the conundrum. This is the story.

Background and the Negotiation Challenge

Abilio dos Santos Diniz, a retail tycoon from São Paulo, Brazil, is the son of a Portuguese immigrant. Diniz's father founded Grupo Pão de Açúcar in 1948 in Brazil. Under Diniz's management, Grupo Pão de Açúcar became Brazil's largest retailer, with revenue of $24.9 billion in 2012. How Diniz got to this point and where the negotiation in question comes from have to do with a French company called Groupe Casino.

The relationship between the two companies began in 1999, when Groupe Casino acquired 24.5% of the voting capital of Grupo Pão de Açúcar for $854 million. In 2000, Diniz transitioned the company into Companhia Brasileira de Distribuição, which became one of the largest retail chains in Brazil. Then in 2005, Diniz sold another large stake to Groupe Casino for an estimated $860 million and subsequently stepped down as CEO. However, he remained on as the chairman of the board. In 2012, Groupo Casino took control of Grupo Pão de Açúcar and Diniz no longer had operational functions within the group but remained as chairman. At this point the relationship between Diniz and Groupo Casino began to sour badly. In 2016, Diniz became a significant shareholder of Carrefour SA, also a French company, and Casino's biggest competitor.[2]

Diniz's relationship with Casino became increasingly belligerent, especially when it came to his relationship with the French retailer's CEO, Jean-Charles Naouri. The fight over control of Brazil's largest retailer, and its 150,000 employees, was at stake. To say that the negotiation had a high public profile was, well, an understatement.

The issue in question was that Diniz had agreed to transition the business over to Naouri at a certain point, but then reconsidered and decided against it. This led to a public disagreement that ended in a fight borne out through the mainstream media and social media. Both men solicited the help of numerous law-yers from across the world, spending millions of dollars to deal with the issue of control of the company. Accusations escalated to claims of corporate espionage. Character assassinations in the press of both men occurred frequently. The *Financial Times* went so far as to call the issue perhaps the biggest cross-continental business dispute in recent history.[3]

The issue was likely to go on for an additional eight years, the length of Diniz's remaining tenure on the board. Diniz had just about resigned himself to that reality – until he sat down with Ury. Then things began to change after a pivotal conversa-tion between the two men.

Preparing to Negotiate

Ury met with Diniz in his living room one afternoon in São Paulo. As they talked, Diniz's young children wandered in and out. Ury inquired in classic advisor fashion, "What is it exactly that you want?" Diniz's response was very focused on the five or six tangible things he sought, such as a good price for his stock, elimination of the three year noncompete clause, and issues pertaining to the corporate headquarters. It was a very matter-of-fact list that would be commonly sought after in these types of negotiations. However, Ury knew that there was almost always another dimension to negotiations – the intangible or psycho-logical realm.[4] He knew he needed to probe there to get to the real root of the problem.

Ury pushed Diniz a bit. "I understand those things, but what do you *really* want?" Diniz looked at him for a while, trying to grasp what Ury was seeking to comprehend. After a bit more explanation from Ury, Diniz said, "Freedom."[5] Ury nodded, feel-ing his question answered. Freedom – in its broadest sense – was the underlying intangible need trying to come through. Having done his homework, Ury knew that Diniz had been kidnapped in 1989 by some urban guerillas.[6] It was a very high-profile situation that was front-page news. If that was not traumatic enough, he was held by his captors in a coffin for a week. Only by a miracle did the police find him. So the concept of freedom was not mentioned casually. It had the deepest of meanings for Diniz.

Ury wanted to make sure he was not reading too much into the word *freedom*. "What does freedom mean to you?" he queried further. This time, Diniz did not need to think. "Freedom to spend time with family and freedom to do business deals, which are the things I love." Ury could certainly resonate with that. He answered, "I am not sure I can get you all of the specific things you mentioned, but maybe I can help with winning you the freedom you want."

Two months later Ury was able to secure a meeting in Paris with a friend and business mentor of Naouri in Paris, an eminent French banker named David de Rothschild. Rothschild sat on the board of Naouri's company. Ury was joined by his colleague David Lax, an experienced business negotiation expert who had been working closely on the case with Ury. This is where the real negotiation began.

The Negotiation

In a private room at an elegant French restaurant the first Monday in September, Rothschild began by asking Ury very simply, "Why are you here?" Ury replied in French, "Parce que la vie est trop courte," meaning "Life is too short." Somewhat puzzled, Rothschild asked, "What do you mean?" Ury continued, "Life is too short for these battles where everyone loses – the protagonists, their families, the employees of the company, even the countries." This situation had become very toxic and was being felt far beyond the two companies. In fact, the ripple effect was so great that the French and Brazilian presidents got involved because it was hampering commercial relations at the governmental level. As Ury portrayed it, "The conflict had achieved mythic proportions."[7]

To this point, there had been eighteen months of negotiation with no movement at all. All that had happened was a hardening of positions, a ratcheting up of the rhetoric, and a lot of money had been spent. Virtually everyone thought the problem could not be solved because the process to that point had all been about someone winning and someone losing. Neither man could afford to lose.

Rothschild was intrigued by what Ury was getting at. "So, how would you approach this?" That was the opening Ury needed. Ury did not get into the details. Instead, he asked for something very simple – agreement on two intangible principles: freedom and dignity.[8] Ury shared that he believed both men wanted to be free to live their lives again and neither wanted, nor could afford, to appear to lose in this scenario. Ury looped back to the concept of dignity and emphasized its critical importance in this case. Rothschild signaled that he understood and would take this to Naouri. Rothschild asked when Ury and Lax were heading back to the US. They explained they were planning to leave the following day. The meeting ended shortly thereafter.

Later that day, Rothschild called Ury back and asked if he could delay his trip and come back to his office the following day because there was more to discuss. Ury and Lax agreed to change their plans. The next day, Ury and Lax met together with Rothschild for a short, 45-minute meeting. Rothschild asked Ury what he really meant by freedom and dignity, and together they crafted a half-dozen deal terms that would reflect those two principles. One of the main issues, for example, was a three-year noncompete clause. Ury explained that given Diniz's age (76), three years was considerable. Previous negotiations had sought to reduce the three-year time period by a third or a half, but the principle of freedom implied zero years – the total elimination of the noncompete clause. The principle of dignity meant that neither party should be perceived as the loser, which was very important since the conflict was so public. Ury and Lax outlined with Rothschild an approach that did not include a single number because, as Ury shared, "Someone will appear to win, and someone will appear to lose, if we use numbers." The voting shares would be traded for nonvoting shares using a 1-for-1 formula with no discount and, hence, no numbers. The intention was to keep the psychological interests front and center.

Having made substantial progress, Ury rerouted himself and flew back to São Paulo instead of the US. He subsequently met with Diniz on Wednesday morning and shared what he had explored with Rothschild. By Friday the parties, with Ury's help, had the outlines of a deal that both men were happy with. Before finalizing everything Ury had asked Diniz's team whether there was anything more they wanted to ask for. They couldn't think of anything. Diniz specifically shared this: "I got everything I wanted, but most importantly, I got my life back."[9] Naouri, Rothschild reported, had also declared his full satisfaction with the agreement. It was a genuine mutual gains agreement with a win as well for the families, the employees, and the larger community.

The principles of freedom and dignity underpinned the document both men signed sitting in a law office in São Paulo. In addition to the agreement, Ury had proposed releasing a joint statement from both men wishing each other well and success into the future. The men agreed.

Ury then went with Diniz and Naouri to the company to share the deal with the top executives. In front of everyone, Diniz and Naouri wished each other well. The media who attended the subsequent press conference could not believe what they were witnessing, but the agreement held.

Later that evening, Ury joined Diniz at his home for dinner. Several dozen lawyers showed up at Diniz's house from around the world to work on arbitration hearings connected to the case. Diniz happily shared word of the agreement, but sadly for them, that was the end of the work on the case.

Lessons Learned

This example demonstrates how quickly a negotiation can escalate when the stakes are high, the process transpires in the public sphere, and both parties need to save face. Without a dramatic reframing, this negotiation would likely have ended in stalemate and with both sides unhappy.

Lesson 1: Dig Down for Intangible Interests Rooted in Psychological Concepts

First, of course, the key to solving this very tough negotiation was to dig down to the roots of the problem, which lay not in money, but in core principles of what made these two men human. Freedom and dignity. All the negative emotions that had spilled into this negotiation were a result of these two needs not being met. In fact, to take that a step further, each man was actively trampling upon the freedom and dignity of the other. Whether this was done willingly or incidentally as a result of the actions taken is immaterial. The impact was the same.

Along with these important psychological issues came a series of assumptions both sides made that fueled the escalatory cycle. As Diniz said to Ury in one of their early conversations, "Maybe I should just resign myself to the fact that I am going to have to fight this until the day I die." This prevailing mindset, along with the lawsuits and other zero-sum ways of thinking, focused on the money and the noncompete clause, which fueled the problem.[9]

Lesson 2: Use of Principles and Objective Criteria

Second, Ury and Lax resisted the trap of centering on the dollars and cents that all the others who previously tried to negotiate this matter focused on. How did they go about doing this? By fixing their minds on principles and objective criteria. As was previously mentioned, the principles of freedom and dignity were critically important. Equally important was using objective criteria, for example the swapping of voting and non-voting shares, so that both men could claim victory and save face.

Lesson 3: Reframing and Pivoting

Finally, this case required Ury holding up a mirror to the participants, reframing the challenge, and pivoting in a different direction. As Ury shared, "If you change the way people see the problem you can change the conversation."[10] The parties had been looking at the problem as a nail and, as such, they all brought their hammers. This would have led to a seemingly never-ending problem that would have cost them all many millions of dollars and left them very unsatisfied in the end. While the reframing alone would not have solved the problem, it opened the door to other possibilities.

Notes

1. Please note that this story appeared in Ury's book *Getting to Yes with Yourself and Other Worthy Opponents*. While the backdrop of the story is the same, the focus and perspective presented herein is distinct.
2. For more information on the background of this situation, please see https://en.wikipedia.org/wiki/Abilio_Diniz
3. For more information on the background of this situation, please see https://www.ft.com/content/cb17619b-9388-3397-ac60-48eae6b56ce2
4. Intangible interests in negotiation have to do with the person and the things that make us human, including respect, dignity, honor, and fear.
5. Interview with William Ury.

6. For more information on this story, please see https://www.nytimes. com/1989/12/31/world/guerrillas-kidnapping-ring-broken-brazil-says.html

7. Interview with William Ury.

8. Interview with William Ury.

9. Interview with William Ury.

10. This is not to suggest that the money was not a key part of this negotiated solution. Rather, it is to say that it was not the key that unlocked the solution in and of itself.

11. Interview with William Ury.

11

Looking under the Hull: How Uncovering Information Led to a New and Better Agreement

Anonymous contribution

There is often a desire on the part of negotiation parties to renegotiate, particularly when they have locked themselves into a long-term contract and a dramatic shock to the landscape occurs. This renegotiation is often not easy, especially when one side is benefiting from the current arrangement. In this case, not only did such a dramatic remaking of the landscape transpire, but new information came to light about the hidden benefits of the current pact.

How was the company on the poor end of the deal able to turn the tide and renegotiate a different deal? Part of the impetus came from a deeper understanding of the previous agreement and hidden benefits to one party. The other part came from a suspect action by the party benefiting from the arrangement and how that flew in the face of what was acceptable from a cultural point of view.

Background and the Negotiation Challenge

This negotiation took place between two companies. The first negotiating party was a major industrial company from the Middle East North Africa (MENA) region called Iron Works (IW). IW was represented by its CEO, Tyler Makin. The second negotiation party was a shipping company called Seabourn Trading (ST), which was based in northern Europe. ST was represented by its CEO, Jan Erlich. This negotiation occurred in the shadow of arbitration – an arbitration Mr. Makin openly concedes his company would have lost.

IW had awarded ST a five-year fixed shipping contract in 2008 prior to the global economic meltdown. IW agreed to pay ST $25 per ton of ore and ST was to transport approximately 2 million tons of that ore per year from Australia to the MENA region. IW would use that ore to make their steel products – the ore represented about 70% of IW's production cost.

The process of getting the ore from Australia was relatively straightforward. ST ships would specifically go to Australia and load up under a Freight on Board (FOB) contract arrangement. This meant that the ships were going there with the explicit purpose and delivering the ore to IW.

IW's problems began when IW had a dispute with their primary ore supplier in Australia.[1] As a result, IW did not have a way to get cargoes of ore onto ST ships until a deal was worked out with them. This issue began to have a ripple effect and certainly impacted IW's relationship with ST because they could not load their ships. Eventually, the dispute was resolved, and IW was able to get their processes moving with ST.

Furthermore, the cost of shipping after the 2008 economic collapse went from $25 per ton to $10 per ton. IW had agreed to pay ST the $25 per ton fixed for a five-year period. The commodities market had simply bottomed out. Makin was getting intense pressure from his board to try to get out from underneath this loss-making contract.

The CEOs met to discuss the situation. Mr. Makin had to make the case to Mr. Erlich that a new contract needed to be hammered out, given the change in circumstances and some new information they had become privy to.

Preparing to Negotiate

Mr. Makin had two objectives as he prepared to try to negotiate a new deal. The first objective was to renegotiate the fixed contract given the high price IW was now paying due to the severe economic circumstances. The second objective he wanted to achieve was to address what he saw as a disparity in the relationship between IW and ST. The disparity occurred because ST was loading its ships from Australia and transporting the ore to IW. Then, ST was reloading their ships again after dropping off the IW shipment with a backhaul, which means taking different materials back in the other direction. Most companies don't do this backhaul, so it was incredibly profitable for ST. The backhaul had previously not been known to Makin and IW, but when he learned of this dynamic Makin felt the value generated by this arrangement should be shared by both parties.

Makin knew that he had a way of revisiting the contract. Since he was having a dispute with his primary ore supplier in Australia, he was unable to get the ore to the ST ships. As such, everything came to a grinding halt. IW explained to ST that they could not perform the contract between the two of them for this reason. Makin knew this would be debilitating for ST and put pressure on them because they constantly had ships that needed to be loaded to complete the backhaul route.

As Makin did his preparation and went through the reasons Erlich might agree to renegotiate, he came up with two in particular. Both of the issues helped to tip the balance of power in the negotiation from being in ST's strong favor to a more symmetrical arrangement. First, IW had hired a forensic accountant to review their books and financial arrangements with all their partners. In the process, the accountant found a minor corruption issue with ST. While this corruption issue had occurred many years in the past, IW leaked this to the press in the country where ST was based. As a European country with a very strong culture of morality and ethics, this became a big stain on ST's reputation. ST wanted the situation resolved as quickly as possible.

The second reason also came as a result of the forensic accountant's analysis. It was also then that they uncovered the backhaul issue that was benefitting ST. The forensic accountant estimated this resulted in an additional profit in the range of $10 to $15 per ton. With such a tremendously valuable contract, ST would be loath to walk away from it.

Makin would have to thread the needle because, while these two things were on his side, he was keenly aware that if he and IW went to arbitration the potential loss, which was very likely, was in the range of $100 million.

From the other perspective, as Erlich thought this through, he too realized there were a number of reasons to renegotiate the contract. He correctly believed that he would win the arbitration case he was bringing against IW and, thus, initially had leverage. As he began down that road, the IW corruption investigation emerged. Coming from a very honor-driven country, ST conducted their own internal investigation and did indeed find there was truth to the claims from IW that a past contractor had taken commissions for placing business with them. While at the time of those contracts this was legal, the laws had subsequently changed, and this action was now considered bribery. ST did not even know about the issue with the contractor, but eventually took responsibility and felt obligated to make it up to IW. Erlich was embarrassed by this personally, and it was very bad publicity for ST. He and his chairman wanted to get this settled and out of the press as soon as possible.

In the end, Erlich's analysis caused him to conclude that the contract with IW was indeed very valuable due to the backhaul issue. Now that the backhaul dynamic was known, the negotiation took on a new feel. ST did not want to lose the deal, and their BATNA of doing sporadic ad hoc shipments of cargo was not preferable because it would impact the exceedingly profitable backhaul business. There were some other companies that needed the same kind of service as IW, but most of those companies were already tied up in long-term contracts.

The Negotiation

When Makin and his lawyers met with Erlich and his lawyers, the negotiation began very badly. The meeting was testy, to say the least, with the lawyers largely hurling accusations at each other. At that meeting Erlich said, "You are not getting out of the contract, and if we need to go to arbitration, so be it."[2] After the meeting ended, Mackin and Erlich decided to go for a drink to try to work things out informally.

As they began to talk, Erlich reiterated the arbitration issue and threat. Mackin knew that he could no longer avoid the renegotiation. Erlich shared that when IW leaked the corruption investigation about ST's company to the papers, everyone, including their chairman, was deeply upset. As such, there was an urgency to deal with this immediately. Mackin recalls Erlich saying, "We are where we are – now let's deal with the issue."[3]

Mackin understood the urgency. Since IW had settled their case with their primary ore supplier this meant that IW no longer had an excuse not to fulfill the original contract at the very inflated price. Ironically, even though they achieved a good settlement with the ore supplier, this solution actually put IW in a weaker position to negotiate the deal with ST. As part of the settlement with the ore supplier, IW entered into a very favorable long-term contract. This gave IW the confidence to do the same with ST and enabled them to offer ST a longer contract than the original five-year deal.

Once the longer contract was put on the table, both parties agreed to drop their respective claims. At that point the tenor changed between them. With the longer-term contract agreed to that mirrored the IW contract with the ore supplier, IW could guarantee ST all the cargoes it needed to secure its profitable backhaul business. In return, ST entered into a new contract with IW based upon current market prices, which were approximately $10 per ton versus the previously agreed upon $25 per ton.

In the end, both sides achieved their goals. IW got out from a debilitating contract. ST got the longevity they desired in the contract and a guarantee that their very profitable backhaul business would continue. Finally, ST was able to rid itself of the bad publicity from the corruption claims and restore its reputation.

Lessons Learned

This case presents some important lessons related to the hidden dimensions of the negotiation. As has been discussed, while it is not uncommon for each party to be working from incomplete information, the case demonstrates what happens when that information is slowly revealed.

Lesson 1: Uncovering New Information and Constantly Assessing a Negotiated Relationship

The first lesson of this negotiation is that one has to keep their eyes and ears open to what is happening as a negotiation evolves and there is a move to the implementation phase. In this scenario, IW had negotiated a deal with ST, but ultimately came to understand that this contract had a much greater benefit to ST as a result of the lucrative backhaul business.

Prior to this new information coming to light, IW did not feel they had much leverage to address the imbalance in the relationship. After learning of this new element, however, IW understood how valuable their contract was with ST and that they had more clout than they previously realized. They used that leverage to actually enlarge the pie and to get ST to revisit the previous deal and to come to a new agreement where they mutually gained.

Lesson 2: Cultural Norms as Levers

The second lesson arises from a key cultural consideration. In this negotiation an issue of potential corruption arose that pushed significantly against the cultural norms of ST. This reputational issue created a sense of urgency to deal with the problem, which brought the parties back to the table. Sometimes understanding how certain elements of culture can aid a negotiation process can be the key to getting people to engage when they otherwise are resisting.[4]

Lesson 3: Sequencing Matters

The third lesson is that of sequencing. There are a few different types of sequencing approaches in negotiation. The first type is within a negotiation and which issues to address first. The second type, which is relevant in this case, is the sequencing of different parallel negotiation processes. In this case, IW's negotiation with ST was held up by a number of factors, the most important of which was the lack of a deal with IW's primary ore supplier. Without the supply-side deal done, IW was not able to finalize an agreement with ST. This proved to be to IW's benefit so they could work through the process with ST, but at a pace that benefitted them. Furthermore, time became a factor in IW's favor, and they were able to manage both processes to their benefit.

Lesson 4: The Ebb and Flow of Internal and External Negotiations

The last lesson here was that, while this negotiation had many moving parts, a critical element was the internal negotiations that each side had to manage. Makin was getting tremendous pressure from his board to renegotiate the poor contract they had agreed to. Further, IW's legal team was taking a very hard line as well. Makin had to manage that, while still finding a way forward with ST.

On the other side of the table, ST was internally struggling with the reputational issues that had been caused by the negative media coverage, resulting in embarrassment to the company's board of directors. ST was in turmoil and the board had begun to micromanage the business – holding monthly meetings with Erlich. They wanted the situation resolved and quickly, which put additional pressure on Erlich as he managed the negotiation process with Mackin.

Notes

1. The ore supplier was the company that took the ore directly out of the ground and brought it the port to be loaded on the ships.
2. Interview with the contributor of the story.
3. Interview with the contributor of the story.
4. It has also been acknowledged that there was an ethical dimension to this problem on both sides. The first was with ST and the contractor issue. While they claimed they were unaware, and it certainly seemed as if this were the case, the fact that it happened should be noted and responsibility taken. The second ethical issue was with IW and their raising of this issue in ST's home country. Certainly, while this did not break any laws, there was an aspect to it that was slightly cunning.

12

When Rushing to Yes Leads to Bigger Problems – but Then a Solution

Based on an interview with Vantage Partners

As you will read in the following case, when a difficult problem arose between two companies involved in a complex partnership, finding a solution involved significantly expanding the scope of the negotiation and broadening the aperture on possible ways to meet each side's interests. With the help of a third party, however, the negotiators ultimately uncovered a collaborative solution.

Background and the Negotiation Challenge

Two companies had entered into a long-term agreement where one agreed to serve as external manufacturing partner to the other. The first company is called Arma and the second, acting as the manufacturer, is called PPM. The agreement came under a great deal of pressure for a number of reasons. After the agreement was signed, Arma found that demand for their products significantly exceeded what they had forecast, and they needed more output from PPM. While in theory that would mean more revenue for both sides, it was not easy for PPM to meet a higher level of demand from the plant they owned that was to produce all products included in the scope of the agreement. At a minimum, doing so would require significant capital investments from PPM, and even with major investments, it was unclear the plant they had agreed would supply product to Arma could meet their needs. In addition to all of this, there were also significant quality and production issues with the plant that came to the surface and needed to be addressed. Finally, while Arma desperately needed more output to keep up with demand, PPM was already failing to meet their *existing* commitment. These failures were resulting in penalties and related fees that had begun accruing shortly after the agreement was signed. This in turn created significant friction at the plant and with the mid- and lower-level employees.

Arma recognized they were hitting a stalemate and needed some help. That is when they decided to bring in Vantage Partners – a consulting firm with expertise in complex partnerships, outsourced manufacturing contracts, and negotiations – to help with the process. It was at this point that a more concerted effort transpired to determine how to best manage all the problems that had emerged from the previous agreement.

Preparing to Negotiate

Due to the fact that Arma brought Vantage in, and were paying them, Arma and Vantage had to persuade PPM to let Vantage come in as a third party to help both sides. PPM was, of course, skeptical. As part of their efforts to persuade PPM of their utility, Vantage proposed to designate a specific member of the Vantage team to be an advocate and point of contact for PPM. PPM's representatives would be able to share confidential information with that Vantage team member and they would discuss what, if anything, could be shared in a joint session or simply as important background that should be kept private. This would give PPM's representatives the ability to express their fears and concerns with a member of the Vantage team and to help them either see the challenge differently or to constructively raise it as part of the process. PPM eventually accepted the offer.

As Vantage began to assist the parties to prepare, they found some very important information to aid the process. Arma explained at the outset that they had a unique and proprietary expertise in manufacturing and yield management. It was evident to the Vantage team that they were very proud of the system, culture, and the people that they had developed. Arma had offered to give PPM a licensing deal without charging them. The idea was that PPM could use the system to solve a number of the problems facing them from the previous agreement. Vantage also proposed exploring a plant within a plant approach. What this meant was that Arma would take over ownership or operation of part of the plant, but not all of it. This type of arrangement is done from time to time, but is often quite complicated.

As Vantage worked with Arma, they quickly discovered other important factors. First, although Arma's system would indeed help address some of the issues at the plant, it was clear that even if they fully implemented the system to its potential, it would still not come close to the capacity Arma needed. There were only so many square feet at this plant, and they could only produce so much.[1] At the very least, this was a partial solution.

Second, when Vantage discussed Arma's system with PPM, they ran into a lot of resistance. After learning about the features of Arma's system, PPM shared that they did not feel Arma's system was much better than their own. In fact, it had already gotten to a point where PPM's representatives became tired of hearing how wonderful Arma's manufacturing process was. Not to mention that if PPM were to take that option forward, Arma's representatives would have to go to the plant and inspect and audit every aspect of the plant in a very intrusive manner.

This all was happening while penalties were accruing. PPM was breaching its supply commitment under the current agreement and was worried that there might be legal implications if an invasive audit of the plant were to be conducted. As Vantage learned, this fear was not unfounded. PPM's representative shared with the Vantage team representative that Arma had previously threatened to sue PPM for undisclosed reasons.

The more that Vantage assessed the capacity at the plant, and the more they looked at Arma's products, the more they came to believe that the plant simply could not meet Arma's demands over the medium and long term. So the Vantage team came up with a number of options based on their conversations with Arma and other research they conducted. These included:

1. A plant-within-a-plant agreement.
2. Invert the arrangement and have Arma be a manufacturer to PPM, but with the one exception for a key product of their own that PPM manufactured at the plant. In that arrangement, Arma would have taken over the rest of the facility and provided some capacity to PPM for a specified period of time.
3. Selling the entire facility to Arma.

This last option was the best for Arma because PPM would exit the plant entirely. The beauty of the last option was that it was much less messy because Arma would have full control of the plant. Arma and Vantage saw this last option as highly unlikely, however, given the resistance from PPM and the fact that they had adamantly rejected the outright sale of the facility in the initial negotiation.

Another part of the calculus was that since both companies were international in scope, it was best to have their production as close to the places where they wanted to distribute the bulk of their product. Ironically, as more details came to light, it was revealed that Arma was in the process of building another plant in the same geographic region. Arma began to do an assessment of which approach made more sense (find a way to buy PPM's plant or continue with their own).

This is where the issue of time entered the equation. As the Vantage team asked Arma's representatives, "What if you take on more capacity? Can you delay breaking ground on this yet to be developed plant and use the money and spend it on an upgrade of the supplier facility? That would give the supplier the short-term capital they need and make it cheaper for you to take over, upgrade the facility, and eventually gain full control."[2] As has previously been articulated, Arma wanted a lot more capacity in the immediate future and PPM did not need much now, but rather wanted to protect their future capacity. PPM was also very reticent about sharing future capacity demands.

Vantage continued to dig into this at a deeper level and assessed this issue from the short, medium, and long term. The pieces began to fit together. Arma had acute needs now to increase their capacity, while PPM desperately wanted to get rid of the penalty fees. PPM was losing money on Arma's business that they had committed to under the supply agreement. PPM also discussed whether there might be actions taken in the midterm. Finally, PPM explained that the best solution might take many years to come to fruition, but that agreement would deal with the underlying issues due to shifting manufacturing from one place to the other.

Negotiation

After some very thorough preparation, the Arma and PPM representatives came together in a joint session facilitated by Vantage. As the Vantage team laid out the importance of the short, medium, and long-term elements, one of the lead people on

PPM's side explained that they were not interested in short-term changes – only in longer-term options. Slightly perplexed by this, a Vantage team member asked why that was the case. PPM's representative shared that from their point of view the real solution lay in the mid to long term. The Vantage partners offered that by also talking about the short term, they could try to give relief to PPM on penalties and help Arma get the level of product they needed. This result would reduce anxiety and pressure and help the parties deal with mid and long term. While PPM's representative was still not sold on the efficacy of this approach, the Vantage team decided to keep trying to nudge the process forward, knowing that the short-term issue would be solved along the way and there would be more opportunity to deal with the mid- and longer-term arrangements.

The Vantage team then laid out the series of options they had worked on in the preparation phase. The Vantage team then asked both teams to go off by themselves, caucus, and discuss the different options presented. Arma's team knew that the best option for them was still an outright purchase of the facility. They also knew PPM had previously said no to that option so they were not hopeful that would materialize. Later that day the PPM team came back and explained, after having reviewed all the options side by side, that they now believed selling Arma the facility outright was their best way forward. Both Arma and Vantage were a bit surprised, but quite happy they all had landed in the same place. Of course, there were many details to be worked out – including valuation, timing, and so on – but they had a deal moving forward that was best for all.

One had to wonder, what changed for PPM where they went from a hard no on the sale of the facility to that becoming their best option? In part, what changed was the framing and the economic reality pressing down upon them. Due to the original agreement and the penalties involved, this sale provided PPM with the ability to do away with significant costs and windup the considerable time they were spending putting out endless fires. This new sale provided PPM with the opportunity to get a significant amount of capital up front as well. They could then deploy these resources away from the region the contracted plant was located in, and toward other regions where they expected more future growth. The bottom line was that the facility was worth more to Arma than PPM.

Lessons Learned

This case demonstrates how a strong desire to get to yes can lead the parties astray. Sometimes parties are so focused on getting to yes that they don't get to the *right* yes and know when a proposed deal might do more harm than good. Thankfully they were able to salvage the relationship and, in the end, renegotiate a deal that better met both sides' interests.

Lesson 1: More Due Diligence and Creative Thinking Could Have Helped Alleviate This Problem from the Start

Arma's future capacity demands were not well understood, and consequently not adequately addressed, in the initial agreement. Moreover, PPM's near- and long-term needs to manufacture their own products in the same plant were not explicitly discussed, nor were the challenges they faced with respect to future capital investments to fund their growth plans. Had a more expansive and transparent negotiation process been used for the first agreement, a major renegotiation might not have been necessary.

In addition, the financial terms of the initial deal – cost-plus and penalties for failing to meet production targets – were very standard in such agreements, but were agreed to without considering how they might create perverse incentives under certain scenarios and various market conditions.

Lesson 2: Changing Circumstances Is Often the Best Way to Change Minds

How to change people's minds in a negotiation is an age-old question. Of course, there are tools at one's disposal, such as persuasion and influence. Sometimes, however, changing circumstances are also necessary to alter the negotiation stance of a slightly intransigent party.

In this instance, the evolution of the deal created the right conditions for PPM to reassess a previously held fear – that selling the plant was not as bad as they had initially considered. In fact, this approach met an interest of theirs (i.e. an infusion of capital) that strategically made sense for them.

Lesson 3: The Role of Process

The final lesson in this case is the role of process. The relationship between Arma and PPM was distrustful, and the negotiation process had become bogged down due to the previous agreement that was floundering. Had they continued down that road, it is likely that the process would not have ended well for either party.

Instead, by bringing in an outside party to help – particularly with the negotiation process itself – the parties were able to orient themselves differently and engage in some creative thinking. Having a menu of options to consider, and initially caucusing individually, aided them in comparing the best options in front of them and to realize there was indeed an optimal solution that existed that met their respective interests.

Notes

1. For a number of reasons, there was no way to expand the footprint of the plant.
2. Interview with Vantage partners.

13

How Interests and Creativity Overcame a Negotiation Gap

Based on an interview with Mark Young

In some negotiations the gap between the needs of the respective negotiators is simply too large to overcome, both financially and with other issues. When this realization sets in on the parties, it is common for all involved to determine that nothing more can be done, and they decide they have no choice but to go their separate ways. This is particularly the case when there is a lack of crossover within the Zone of Possible Agreement (ZOPA).

Such was the scenario in this case, until the parties involved altered their way of thinking by removing themselves directly from the negotiation process and designating an informal working group to take over and to determine what they could create that might satisfy the different needs the parties had. Ultimately when the parties involved set up such a group, they came to realize that other factors they had not previously considered were driving the deal. With that insight, they were able to overcome the perceived gaps and find a creative solution that worked for all the parties.

Background and the Negotiation Challenge

In 1993, as part of the reunification of East and West Germany and the subsequent privatization of many industries, the Agency in Trust (AT) decided to sell the famous Deutsche Film-Aktiengesellschaft (DEFA) Studio. DEFA was the birthplace of the German film industry and where Fritz Lang and Marlene Dietrich, among many others, began their careers and became stars. The studio sat on a 40-hectare plot of land[1] with a very large portion of the area still undeveloped. The other party to the negotiation was the French company Compagnie Générale des Eaux (CGE), which today is known as Vivendi.

Dr. Gert Schmidt was department head for AT. He was given the mandate of selling all of the companies and closing down the entire studio portfolio within a six-week time frame. If he were able to accomplish that feat within the time frame, he would be given a substantial bonus. Interestingly, he did not initially need payment for the deal within those six weeks, but he did have to reach a general agreement for the income to count toward his bonus. Dr. Schmidt was also one of the few former East German officials in management at the company. This background would become important in the negotiation for a number of reasons that will be discussed later.

Ivan Laurier was the vice president of International Acquisitions at CGE. At the time of this negotiation, Mr. Laurier had 10 years of experience in making international acquisitions in a variety of industries. Mr. Laurier came to Berlin in order to conduct the negotiations to buy the company that owned DEFA studios. Laurier was unclear on where the process would lead and how good a deal this was for the company, but he was interested in exploring the possibilities.

Preparing to Negotiate

For both of the parties to the negotiation, there was a lot of uncertainty involved. As CGE and Laurier analyzed the situation, they wanted to take things slowly to make certain the deal was right for them. In particular, they were uncertain how they would use the vast plot of land, but they were clear about one thing. The studio would help their profile across Europe as they continued developing their foothold in the filmmaking industry. Mr. Laurier also knew that property in East Germany after the reunification was selling fast and this particular venue held sentimental value for many Germans. Finally, after receiving DEFA's initial offer, Laurier was very skeptical a deal could be reached since there was a significant gap in the ZOPA.

Laurier began his preparation with some unease, considering he was handed a situation where his colleagues seemed overly eager for a deal. Laurier's boss had signed a letter of intent with CGE to buy DEFA and Laurier was forced to attend a joint press conference when he arrived before he could do his own due diligence (much more research was needed from his point of view). In addition, CGE was already overextended in their acquisitions and intercompany borrowing at CGE was very expensive.

Laurier's staff conducted an initial earnings-based cash flow valuation of the companies and recommended that CGE not pay more than 35 million euros for DEFA. They also recommended this be paid out over a few years. Laurier's boss has explained to him that he could pay up to 50 million euros, but that seemed very unrealistic to Laurier based on his own information. There was one critical place where Laurier was fully onboard, however – he saw the strategic value of DEFA for CGE's overall business plan and future focus.

There was one other key issue Laurier needed to be aware of during this negotiation that he contemplated as he prepared to engage. While he did not want to rush, there was indeed time pressure on him as well. CGE had recently signed a contract for a 100-million-euro European film project, subsidized by the European Union (EU), to commence by the end of the year. Purchasing DEFA would help greatly with this endeavor – particularly given its strong brand. The only other way to realize their strategic goals related to filmmaking would be to create a new studio on a previously unused site. This BATNA, while possible, would prove to be time-consuming, expensive, and less desirable than reaching a deal with DEFA.

On the other side of the table was Mr. Schmidt. Schmidt had the unenviable task of selling a cultural icon and important entity to the German state in a time of great turmoil. If he sold it to the wrong entity, or for a deal he could not justify, he knew this would be a public relations nightmare.

As is common in many negotiations, Schmidt had his company's interests to consider as well as his own personal interests. When Schmidt was given his mandate, he was told that if he were to be able to sell the company within six weeks he would get a significant bonus. He was also given other parameters listed below that might have felt as if they ran counter to a quick sell.

The first parameter was the sale price. Schmidt was given an internal asset-based valuation that showed the company to be worth at least 60 million euros. Liquidation, with the sale of all assets, would net about 30 million euros for AT.

The second parameter Schmidt had to meet was that all AT sales contracts had to include guarantees by the investor to maintain a certain percentage of jobs and to make suitable capital investments. Of the 1,100 employees working at DEFA at the time, Schmidt was told to preserve as many jobs as possible. Schmidt determined that his goal would be to retain at least 800 people for a minimum of 5 years.

The final parameter Schmidt was working under was to make absolutely certain that CGE continue to develop DEFA as a film business. Schmidt knew that the large plot of land on which DEFA stood was very valuable and several developers had made substantial offers to buy it and turn it into apartments and office space. This would be a political disaster for AT and would confirm everyone's worst fears that most investors were only interested in property speculation. Schmidt was very skeptical of CGE in this regard, given that they were primarily a diversified water utility company, and not a film studio.

Lastly, Schmidt was dealing with all of this against a backdrop of internal turmoil at AT. Numerous layoffs and other scandals had been bubbling up that engulfed AT in chaos. While Schmidt did have another offer from a filmmaking company in Germany, it was a rather dubious one and not a very good BATNA should things fall apart with CGE.

The Negotiation

As the negotiations commenced in Berlin a number of issues rose to the surface immediately. The first issue that had to be addressed was AT's concern about CGE's intentions and their plans for DEFA. Since CGE was primarily a diversified water utility company, AT wanted to know why they were so interested in purchasing the studio and the land. As was previously mentioned, it was critical to AT that the studio be preserved and used into the future for film development. Early on in the process Mr. Laurier was able to assure Mr. Schmidt about CGE's intentions – including a discussion of their new film business and sharing the fact that they had signed a contract with the EU. Further, Mr. Laurier was able to convince Mr. Schmidt about CGE's objectives when he explained that they were really not that interested in the developable land connected to the studio.

Of course, they would agree to take it on as part of the deal, but it was clear that it was more of a potential challenge than benefit.

The second issue that took center stage in the negotiation was the timing of the sale. On numerous occasions, Mr. Schmidt emphasized the importance of signing the contract within six weeks. Initially, it was unclear to Mr. Laurier why this was so critical to Mr. Schmidt and he did not feel that it was appropriate to ask directly. Eventually, through back channel investigations, Mr. Laurier came to understand that there was a bonus in it for Mr. Schmidt if the deal was signed in that time frame. Fortunately, all of the details on the final agreement did not need to be solidified within this six-week time period. This nuance gave the parties the ability to agree in principle, but then slow the process down so that Mr. Laurier could do his due diligence in a comfortable manner.

The final, and perhaps most important, element of the negotiation was the price gap between the parties. This financial chasm was unlikely to be bridged without really understanding the interests of all involved and coming up with a creative option that met everyone's needs. Initially the gap between what AT was seeking and what CGE was willing to pay was significant. CGE was willing to spend up to 30 million, while the target for AT was of 60 million. After considerable back and forth with little progress, Schmidt and Laurier decided to create a collaborative working group that unearthed quite a bit of common ground— helping to enlarge the pie.

A key sticking point that kept arising was the land, which was very valuable, oversized, and totally unnecessary for making movies. The parties eventually reached an arrangement to allow CGE the ability to sell the undeveloped land off piece by piece, with a so-called "clawback" provision. The clawback provision provided for 50% of the proceeds of each parcel of land sold going to AT. This creative solution effectively monetized the deal breaker and created enough resources for both parties to gain and claim victory to their respective constituents.

Lessons Learned

When there is an iconic entity involved in a negotiation the outcome takes on tremendous importance because of the symbolism involved. This was certainly the situation in this example and, when coupled with the tense cultural backdrop of the companies involved, the odds of reaching an agreement seemed almost insurmountable. That is, until the parties used the tactics below and cleverly worked their way through the negotiation problem.

Lesson 1: Separating the Relationship/ Cultural Issues from the Problem

Difficult relationship issues underpinned the negotiations from the beginning, mostly of a cultural nature between CGE (French) and AT (East German). These two countries had a history of tense relations, with each possessing very different cultural norms when it comes to negotiation. The French tend to be more nuanced, circuitous, and diplomatic in their approach, while the East Germans are more direct and logical. Eventually, these were successfully put aside by Laurier and Schmidt to focus on the content of crafting the deal. The key to separating the cultural constraints from the negotiation was to create a working group – away from the two principals – which improved the climate considerably and helped the parties stay focused on the content of the process.

Lesson 2: Not Getting Fixated on Price Helped Generate Creativity

A central lesson to this case was not getting fixated on the overall price, but understanding the deal from a bigger picture point of view. When the parties shifted away from the price, they were able to get into some creative thinking processes that helped them enlarge the pie.

To accomplish the aforementioned task, the parties began to conceptualize the deal and structure in three nested circles. The studio was the first circle; it was at the center and needed to be preserved. Both sides concurred about that. The second circle was the ring around the studio that would comprise buildings and offices that would support the moviemaking endeavors of CGE. The third and final external circle was the developable land that lay on the outskirts of the property. By working out an arrangement that allowed CGE to sell off the properties in that circle piece by piece, with a clawback provision of 50% of the proceeds for AT, the parties were able to monetize what might have become a deal breaker. This also helped CGE convince AT of their seriousness related to the moviemaking industry. Finally, this unlocked the ability of CGE to apply for government subsidies and investment credits to aid in their moviemaking.

Lesson 3: Grasping the Varied Interests Involved

There were many varied interests involved in this negotiation, and they were fundamental to bridging the gaps in this negotiation. When those interests were put on the table and discussed in depth, the parties were able to overcome numerous roadblocks. From a personal interest in getting a deal done within a certain time frame, to a critical need to preserve DEFA, to the ability to use valuable but nonessential property to bridge the financial gaps, interests paved the way for a deal when there was significant skepticism as to whether one would happen at all.

Lesson 4: Guarding against Taboos and Helping the Other Save Face

One of the important lessons from this case was to guard against certain taboos and to enable AT to save face as part of the agreement. A deal breaker for AT was a developer coming in and not preserving the iconic DEFA studio. AT was a steward of a critical part of German history and needed to be able to show how they protected it in any deal. Without a recognition by CGE of how important this was for AT, they would not have been able to save face with the public.

Note

1. One hectare is approximately 2.5 acres of land. So the parcel of land in questions was approximately 100 acres.

14

Power Begets Power Begets Power

Based on an interview with Steven Hauck

As has been previously mentioned, power is one of the most difficult issues to deal with in negotiation. Often it can be debilitating when a negotiator is up against a power asymmetry. Sometimes it feels as if the only action possible is to throw up one's hands and say, "Please just give me something from this negotiation."

However, power in negotiation is far more complex than this straightforward perspective and is something to be wielded very carefully. As Lucius Annaeus Seneca reminds us, "He who has great power should use it lightly."[1] Why would Seneca state that? Well, when a negotiator possesses power they often don't think about a time when they might not have it and what would happen if the tables were turned. Surprisingly this happens quite often in negotiation – one minute a negotiator is in a power position and the next minute they are not. As this case exhibits, if a negotiator does not wield their power carefully, and in a manner that does not damage the relationship, they may very well suffer the consequences at a later date.

Background and the Negotiation Challenge

In this case, the person involved, named Steve, had begun a business, but had some early struggles that necessitated funding to keep the company going. The business was related to the insurance industry and an innovative way to support insurance agents in their work. Eventually, the business did very well for many years and then was bought by a larger company, but the early period was fraught with challenges.

One challenge in particular was a negotiation that Steve termed a "deal he did with the devil." In the moment the deal was painful, but in the end it turned out to be an amazing deal for him and his company. The terms of the deal initially were dictated by the other party, named Pierre.

The specific negotiation challenge that Steve had to address was an infusion of cash in order to meet payroll. Steve did not have many options, so he turned to Pierre to provide his company with the necessary capital. Pierre also surmised that Steve did not have many other options. As part of the initial proposal, Pierre asked Steve to pivot the business to him and he would give them $1 million to keep them going for 6 months. In return, Pierre wanted warrants that equaled 70% of the company.

Steve reviewed his options – which were very limited – and realized he had little leverage. As a counter proposal he decided to ask for $1.2 million in return for 66% of the company. Pierre had anchored the negotiation with an aspirational offer and quickly agreed because it was still a tremendous deal for him. Pierre knew he had the power in this situation and took full advantage of it by what he sought and ultimately achieved. But at what cost? Little did Pierre know that another negotiation would need to transpire in the not too distant future.

Preparing to Negotiate

There was very little preparation in the first negotiation. Pierre had Steve and his company over a proverbial barrel and took full advantage of the situation. Steve also knew that if Pierre exercised the warrants, he would have a significant controlling interest in the company.

After a few years Steve's company was thriving and in a much different position. One day Pierre called Steve on the phone and sought to do another deal. Steve began to wonder what had changed. Eventually, through some sleuthing, Steve came to understand why Pierre wanted a new deal and that the dynamics had shifted – this time dramatically in his favor.

The difference this time around was that Pierre had decided to take his company public. Pierre personally stood to make much more money than what he would have made through Steve's company. On Pierre's balance sheet, however, he had greater than 10% holdings, which he could not have before going public. Thus he had to liquidate his warrants in Steve's business. Given that reality, Steve knew he could now dictate the price to Pierre, and he was able to buy the warrants back for pennies on the dollar. Since Steve's company was in a much better financial situation the tides had indeed turned.

The Negotiation

When Steve received the phone call from Pierre telling him that he needed to divest from Steve's company he stepped back to the balcony and thought strategically about the big picture. Pierre again tried to frame the negotiation to gain favorable terms. Steve, however, was not going to be anchored by Pierre's framing this time. Since Steve had come to understand what was motivating Pierre, he knew that Pierre needed the deal much more than he did.

The more Steve thought about the situation, the more he concluded that he basically had the ability to ask for whatever he wanted since Pierre stood to make much more from taking his company public than staying invested in Steve's company. Furthermore, the fact that Pierre had taken full advantage of the previous negotiation and his power nudged Steve in the same direction. As Steve recalled, "If he (Pierre) wasn't so greedy and had to have a controlling interest and had he not been so ruthless in the original negotiation, we would definitely have been more generous and wanted to work more collaboratively. It was hard to do that, however, given what he had done to us initially."[2]

In the end, Pierre agreed to what Steve asked because it made so much financial sense for him to do so. Pierre was not happy about the terms, but came to the realization that this deal was a result of his own actions in the first negotiation. He was going to have to accept Steve's terms and take the lesson related to power with him into the future.

The complete reversal of leverage astounded both parties and breathed new life into Steve's company. This change, and the unencumbered company, ultimately led Steve to take things in a different direction and to sell the company in the future for a sizable profit.

Lessons Learned

This case study is a classic case of a power play by one side over the other. The problem, of course, is that eventually the power asymmetry changed, setting the stage for a reversal of fortunes.

Lesson 1: Wielding Power and Leverage

This case is first and foremost about negotiating with power and how to do so effectively. As we witnessed herein, in the initial negotiation Pierre had all the power and wielded it to its maximum capacity. He took advantage of the situation down to the last nickel and approached the scenario in a draconian manner. He was not concerned about the implications of doing so.

When the situation changed and the shoe was on the other foot, Pierre paid for such a heavy-handed approach. As Steve recounted, had Pierre approached the situation to get a good deal, but not take maximum advantage, he would have been more gracious on their end. This aligns with the famous quote from John Paul Getty "My father said, 'You must never try to make all the money that's in a deal. Let the other fellow make some money too, because if you have a reputation for always making all the money, you won't have many deals.'"[3] Since Pierre exercised his power completely, Steve felt little to no sympathy when he was forced to divest.

The lesson for negotiators is to wield their power carefully and to remember that there may be an instance in the future where the power asymmetry has flipped. As a general rule of thumb, negotiators should certainly strive to do well for themselves, but they should watch the line where they are simply taking advantage of the other negotiator and damaging the relationship. This is particularly important even when a negotiator thinks they might not negotiate with the other person in the future. Remember, the world is a small place and, as a negotiator, your reputation follows you around.

Lesson 2: A Lot of Negotiation Is Out of Our Hands

As Steve mentioned, the initial deal was a deal with the devil that they had to make to keep the doors open in their fledgling startup.

However, due to unforeseen circumstances and luck, the tides turned, and Steve held all the power in the second negotiation.

What is useful about this is to recognize that a lot of negotiation is out of our control. Sometimes circumstances change and we are given a completely new set of variables to deal with. Good negotiators expect the unexpected and act accordingly with an adaptable mindset. If you sense there is even the slimmest possibility you will be negotiating with your counterpart in the future, factor that it into your decision making.

Lesson 3: Short-Term Gain at the Expense of the Long Term

A theme throughout the book has been to manage the need for short-term gains while preserving the long-term relationship. In this example, Pierre took every last morsel of the deal and let the short term push aside the long term. Even though a negotiator may have the ability to take that approach, they should certainly ask themselves if it is wise. The worst-case scenario should always be conscious somewhere in your mind.

In the end, doing damage in a negotiation to those on the receiving end is self-defeating behavior. This is the case if another negotiation is in the offing, but also simply from a reputational perspective.

Notes

1. Quote can be found here: https://www.brainyquote.com/topics/great-power-quotes
2. Interview with Steven Hauck.
3. J. Paul Getty, cited in Alison Branagan, *Making Sense of Business: A No-Nonsense Guide to Business Skills* (London: Kogan Page, 2009), p. 136.

15

All in the Family: Business Negotiations with Baggage

Based on an interview with Geurt Jan De Haus

Family. Business. Two words that often go together, but sometimes don't integrate well. The problem is that family businesses are often run more like a family and less like a business. As a result, there is a lot of confusion on how to structure the business, assess the outcomes, and manage complicated relationships. As you might have guessed, all of these things and more require vast amounts of negotiation.

Negotiations in this context are often more complicated than simple business negotiations. There are layers of relationships intertwined, various family members involved, and long histories that can greatly conflate matters.

Such was the situation in this example. The familial dynamics were very strong, and there was a lot of relational baggage that became woven into the handing over of the business from one generation to the next. However, with the help of an outside consultant, a father and son were able to work through some difficult issues and find a way to create a well-thought-out succession plan.

Background and the Negotiation Challenge

The story begins with a father, Marcel, who had started a successful business selling medical equipment in Europe. The company was approaching 30 years in business, and there was one partner whom Marcel was able to eventually buy out. Buying his partner out was important for Marcel because he saw this as a family business and really did not want to sell it to others. Like many fathers, Marcel wanted to pass his hard work and the spoils of his labor onto his children and have them follow in his footsteps. Of Marcel's three children, one of his sons, Louis, had expressed an interest in coming in and taking over the business as his father considered retirement. The most important questions concerned what the transition would look like and how the two would negotiate their way through some of the difficult issues involved given their challenging personal history with each other.

As Marcel and Louis sat down to try to sort out a number of the issues in front of them, they quickly became deadlocked. While Marcel wanted to hand the business over to Louis, they had a lot of problems working together. Their somewhat tense relationship degenerated into frustration and fights. They both wondered to themselves how the business could be handed over given the difficult relationship that existed and the different visions each held about the future.

Although he did not have experience in medical supply sales, Louis had been working for the past 15 years in another industry. He had been promoted numerous times and eventually was put in charge of running a medium-size business, which operated internationally. He did so very successfully and, frankly, did not need to make changes to his life unless it made sense.

Preparing to Negotiate

When Marcel and Louis started to talk about Louis coming into the business, and getting down to the details, the negotiation became very delicate and sensitive for both men. The negotiation was positional, with each accusing the other of the wrongdoing. Despite this dynamic, both Marcel and Louis tried numerous times to work through the situation themselves, but were caught in an escalatory spiral that they could not get out of without some help. It was at that point that they finally called in a consultant named Geurt.

Geurt met with each of them individually so he could understand the situation from their respective perspectives. What he heard from each of them individually was that this was a very emotional scenario with a lot of underlying dimensions. As Louis explained, "There were many minor things that happened over the years that went unaddressed, and they now were creating much bigger issues."[1] As but one example of this dynamic, both men confidentially shared with Geurt that they craved credit for what they had accomplished. Marcel lamented that nobody in the family seemed to recognize all the hard work he had put in over the years to build the company. He also did not think that Louis appreciated all he had done for him. Similarly, Louis divulged to Geurt that he had the perception that nothing he ever did was good enough in his father's eyes and that his father had a pretty big ego. At one point in their previous meeting Louis even declared to Marcel "I am not, in your eyes, good enough. Now you need me, and I still need to do things your way!"[2] In short, both were feeling disrespected due to past interactions and a lack of recognition from the other. The future of the business was in serious jeopardy.

One other important factor came to the forefront during their conversation with Geurt. It was clear that Marcel and

Louis's negotiation styles clashed. As is often the case, the apple did not fall far from the tree and both were very competitive personalities. They did not know how to stop the escalation once it started. They were both high on asserting for their own needs, but really struggled to put themselves in the other person's shoes.

The Negotiation

When the parties eventually came together with Geurt it was clear that their similar personalities and negotiation styles were a big part of the challenge. This almost immediately manifested itself in a difficult conversation about their respective BATNAs. For Marcel, his BATNA was not good given that he desperately wanted to keep the business in the family and eventually hand it over to his son. He could not imagine another idea or BATNA, even though he had other children. The problem was that none of his other children were very interested in getting into the business. For Louis, his view at the outset was that his father needed him from a business perspective – he did not need his father. Louis had his career and did not need to make any change. He had a good BATNA as he entered the negotiation.

As Geurt listened to the back and forth, two key questions came to mind that he knew he needed answered so he could proceed. He felt it was critical to get these questions on the table early on: Are you willing to negotiate this issue? and Are you ready to do so?[3] Why were these questions so important? As Geurt shared, "The question of are you willing to negotiate went to the issue of interest and goals. Were the parties' interests met by working together and were their goals aligned with this? The other question, are you ready, went to their mindset and desire. Were they willing to put in the time and effort needed to deal with this challenge? Mentally, were they in a space where they could really try to make this work?"[4]

These questions put the parties' emotions on the table in a roundabout manner and created a conversation centered on this core element of the negotiation. Marcel began very emotionally – he expressed significant frustration and anger about the discussions to date. As Geurt elucidated, "He put much of the blame on himself and was feeling these emotions because he was not able to fix this problem himself."[5] After listening to his father, Louis very candidly expressed a willing to discuss the core issues, but he was also reticent about whether he was ready.

With both parties at least willing, Geurt then asked each party what their preferred outcome would be. He was trying to nudge them toward what readiness might look like and create a positive tone and attitude. Marcel's preferred outcome was that Louis come in and play an important role right away, but he explained he was not ready to give up complete control. Hearing that helped Louis feel respected and to grasp that he would be moving toward where he wanted to be. Geurt began to see changes shortly thereafter. The tone of the conversation shifted, and a new level of trust in him and in each other began to peek through. Put differently, they were beginning to deal productively with the past and the current negotiation problem and learning skills to manage the future.

As the three of them looked back at their past together, and then gazed to the future, they began to discuss common interests as well as those points where they differed. They eventually went back to the emotional discussions they previously had that were characterized by a lack of respect toward each other. Marcel and Louis began to view those conversations differently, this time through a positive frame where they were able to empathize with each other in a way that had not previously happened. Marcel and Louis admitted that there was something bothering them from the past in how they dealt with the other. Marcel confessed that, in the heat of the moment, neither of them understood how their words were perceived by the other party. They could now clearly see how they had harmed the other. Shame and forgiveness emerged for both of them.

This mutual acknowledgment enabled other baggage to come out. Louis shared that he missed his father being around when he was younger and that he needed positive feedback – not just negative input, telling him what he was doing wrong. Marcel acknowledged that he understood and then shared that he had hoped for more credit from his family in building up the company over many years. The emotional bond that had been lacking for so long was beginning to show itself.

At this point Geurt felt he could ask a new critical question. "How can you now move to options where a proper transfer can occur?"[6] Marcel explained that he trusted Louis, but he would feel more comfortable with a slow transfer period. He explained to Louis that there were many nuances to the business, and he would like the opportunity to help him. All the while Marcel would gradually transition out. Louis agreed and they landed on a two-year arrangement for that transition.

Marcel promised he would not micromanage the process and the two developed strict rules of cooperation. This helped Louis to know what he was responsible for and places where they would consult each other. This progress made it possible to work through other important details, including shareholder ownership and the role of other family members.

Lessons Learned

As the reader can envisage from this case, when it comes to family business negotiations there is a lot to know and a lot to learn. The example herein illuminates many key lessons that should help others in a similar situation.

Lesson 1: The Readiness and Willingness Check

Early on when Geurt came into the process the situation looked rather bleak. He gave a lot of thought to where to begin. He realized that he needed to gauge the parties' interests, goals, desires, and frame of mind to work through these issues. As such, he asked them if they were willing to do this. In other words, were their interest and goals aligned with where they collectively wanted to go? That was, however, not enough. Being willing was one thing, but being ready was another. Are you in the right frame of mind and do you have the desire to put in the hard work? was the follow-on question. Both men explained initially that they were willing, but Louis was not quite ready. This honest assessment helped to pinpoint that there was something that needed attention before they could proceed.

Lesson 2: Moving from Competition to Collaboration

Marcel and Louis found themselves in a classic negative spiral due to their competitive negotiation styles. Empathy was the only way out. They had to find a way to put themselves in the other person's shoes. When they did that they could no longer stay angry at each other. Furthermore, by empathizing they naturally moved into a conversation about the emotions that lay at the heart of their damaged relationship and the negotiation process.

As they unpacked their emotions, they began to focus less on positions and more on interests. Geurt asked them to engage in a short but simple exercise – think about your interests and how to share them, but also what you think the interests of the other party are and why those might be so important to them. This straightforward exercise had a big impact, naturally leading to the transition option and the underlying details involved.

Lesson 3: The Intent and Impact Problem

There is a common but often hidden dimension to negotiation called the intent and impact problem. Marcel and Louis suffered from it. Much of the time they would take actions in their negotiations with a certain intention – trying to be constructive and positive. However, the impact on the other, due to the destructive underlying relationship, was always taken as negative. Until they were able to address these emotional issues directly, this would not change. When they addressed the relationship effectively, the assumptions that went along with the intent and impact problem disappeared. It was at that point that they could have much more useful conversations that led to a lasting solution.

Notes

1. Interview with Geurt de Haus.
2. Interview with Geurt de Haus.
3. Interview with Geurt de Haus.
4. Interview with Geurt de Haus.
5. Interview with Geurt de Haus.
6. Interview with Geurt de Haus.

16

When You Hit a Problem, Think to Restructure Instead of Walking Away

Based on an interview with David Lithwick

When most people run into a significant problem in negotiation, their first thought is often just to walk away. That is a very normal response, and yet by walking away they may be missing an opportunity to salvage the situation for the betterment of all involved. Thus instead of walking away, another approach is to think about the specific negotiation problem and try to handle it differently. Along those lines, a useful strategy to consider is restructuring the deal so it takes on a different form and meets the underlying interests of those involved.

One of the issues that gets in the way of restructuring a deal is the problem of precedent. When deals are constructed in a certain manner in a particular industry it is sometimes problematic to move away from that approach. What is familiar is often comforting, but also limiting.

In the case below, not only did the negotiators involved run into a significant problem, but if they did not restructure the deal, the relationship would have been permanently lost and the project in question would have fallen well behind schedule. Add to this dilemma the issue of culture, which was a core factor in this situation, and there are a series of interesting issues that had to be addressed for both parties to ultimately gain from the negotiation. Let's look at what they did to overcome all of these obstacles and still find a mutually agreeable way forward.

Background and the Negotiation Challenge

Aaron worked as the chief technology officer at CXX Technologies, based in Toronto, Canada. This is the story of how CXX Technologies negotiated with partners to create the world's smallest virtual laser keyboard that can be Bluetoothed as a human interface device (HID). This laser keyboard projects a full-sized keyboard onto any flat surface, allowing users to type at the speed of a regular keyboard. CXX continues to explore and work with major manufacturers on embedded applications for its virtual laser touch projection products.

Due to the cost of developing this laser technology in 2012 CXX sought to negotiate a manufacturing deal with a company in China, called Manufix. CXX went to China because it was the most cost-effective way to manufacture the product and because Manufix claimed they had developed an expertise specifically in manufacturing technology that would work for this particular product.

After some exploration and investigation, CXX began down the road of hiring Manufix to do the work of manufacturing the laser keyboard. To initiate the process Aaron went to China to explore the situation in depth and make certain that Manufix could indeed do the work to build the device. After all, this was a very technical project. Aaron was met with many assurances, including the hiring of a professor as part of the Manufix team who was an "expert" on the subject and possessed an enthusiasm for the work. The phrase "can do, can do" was uttered frequently.

Upon his return to Toronto, Aaron was initially satisfied with what he saw. He subsequently negotiated a contract that gave Manufix an initial payment up front of $100,000 in order to get the product development under way and into a proof of concept phase. As Aaron had come to learn, this was standard practice when it came to products such as this, and when working with a company based in China. The contract was also structured in such a manner that Manufix was required to reach a series of milestones by certain dates so both parties knew the project was on track. When they had achieved those milestones, they would continue on to the next stages of development and receive the next series of payments.

The agreed-upon process went on for approximately a year. During that time Aaron kept noticing that deliverables were slipping, and excuses were becoming more frequent. Despite these failings, Manufix was pushing hard for their next payment. They felt they were entitled to it. Aaron and CXX disagreed with them and explained that they had not done the statement of work specified in the contract, and until they did, there would be no further payments. In response, Manufix did not want to put in any more work until they were paid. Clearly the parties had reached an impasse with no clear path ahead.

Aaron sat in his office overlooking a park and all he could think to do was scrap the relationship and start over. This would set him back considerably, but what else could he do?

Preparing to Negotiate

As Aaron turned back from his window, he thought to himself that there had to be another option than exercising his BATNA and changing manufacturers. His timeline and budget would be severely compromised if he made that shift.

Aaron called in his team to brainstorm. They all knew that a big part of the problem was the lump sum being paid, the milestones not being reached, and the lack of accountability from Manufix. As Aaron said to his colleagues, "We are not going to take this approach going forward. We could walk away and find another manufacturer, but that would set everything back badly. So what other arrangement could we come up with?"[1] As they thought together and started throwing ideas around, one person asked if they could restructure the contract. That was the first time this option had come up.

This conversation pushed them to discuss whether they had confidence in Manufix to do the job they were hired to do. There were certain aspects of the project that Manufix seemed capable of doing, but there was a heavy dose of skepticism on the part of the team that they could do everything. So did they need to get rid of them? Or was there another way forward to try to guarantee progress?

As was previously mentioned, the norm with these kinds of contracts was a lump sum approach with milestones. Typically, money was given up front to cover initial costs and then, when the milestones were achieved, the next payment was made until the final product was ready for production. What Aaron decided upon was a new and different structure – one where CXX would give as little money as possible up front and then incentivize Manufix to get to the production phase. However, CXX would also insist on getting Manufix some help in the places where they had demonstrated that they were not competent – namely the laser technology component.

Aaron and his team also knew they had to make it a take-it-or-leave-it offer because of what had happened in the past. The reality was they were behind schedule and would need to move quickly to find another manufacturer should Manufix object and try to drag out the negotiations.

From Manufix's perspective, they had a number of interests in the negotiation. It was clear that they wanted to make a significant profit, which prevented them from looking at solutions that would cost them more money. This limited their creativity and out-of-the-box thinking. They also wanted this project to be a success so they could promote themselves as being on the cutting edge of developing and manufacturing innovative technology. This project, if it went well, would be a stepping stone to further success.

The Negotiation

When the parties came together to renegotiate the deal, CXX laid out the situation from their point of view. Manufix was not performing as they had promised, and CXX was either going to make a change to a different contract manufacturer or they were going to strike a new, incentivized deal. The proposed deal was as follows:

1. CXX would pay Manufix for their costs incurred on the development upon them producing payment receipts.
2. Once Manufix succeeded in development and started manufacturing, they would get paid a royalty on each unit sold. The philosophy behind the new deal was that if CXX succeeded then Manufix succeeded. All boats would rise in this equation. This provision would tie Manufix to the success plan and incentivize them to make the product, to do it as quickly as they could, and only then would they get a return on their money.
3. CXX would bring in a laser specialty company from Taiwan, called Lazo, to supplement the work related to the laser development element of the project since Manufix was lacking this expertise.

When CXX suggested this change to the arrangement Manufix ultimately agreed, but with hesitations. Manufix could not admit they did not know how to complete the project because it would cause them a loss of face. As Aaron recounted, "Companies in China are often very good at saying we 'can do' but not very good at innovation and research and development which they have not done before. It was fairly clear to us they could not do that aspect of the work, but they could not admit it openly for cultural reasons."[2] There were subtle indications that Manufix understood the magnitude of the problem. As just one example, Manufix laid off a number of employees just prior to this critical juncture. To Aaron this was seen as an admission of a significant problem. Fortunately, Aaron was keen enough to observe this dynamic, which is why he brought in Lazo. Without the addition of Lazo the job simply would not have gotten done.

The new deal also hinged on CXX's key interest of managing risk and Manufix letting go of their singular desire to make money just on the research and development. CXX needed Manufix to shift their way of thinking and to view the development and success of this product as a joint venture. CXX had assumed all the risk the first time around, but were not prepared to take all that on in the renegotiation. As Aaron explained, "Manufix could not get the job done alone so we needed a new arrangement that protected us – one where they equally would share in both the risk and reward."[3]

Manufix agreed to the deal, submitted their exact costs, and also consented to have Lazo join the process. Manufix did not put up resistance to Lazo being involved because they wanted the end result of the royalties and the respect of developing an advanced innovative technology product. Manufix knew this deal would show their prowess in the technology field and would enhance their entire portfolio.

Aaron was happy with the end result – CXX did get the project done under this new arrangement. It took another year to complete with a total cost of over $500,000. After the product was developed there was a lot more research and development to be done because CXX wanted to create the next generation of the technology for phones and other small devices. Further negotiations happened between the two and a number of other products have been completed. Manufix made a solid profit on these deals, and they were able to leverage the work to get significantly more business in the future from other companies.

Lessons Learned

It is not uncommon for a negotiated agreement to be reached only to encounter problems during the implementation phase of the process. When this occurs, people's first inclination is to walk away and find another partner. What this case demonstrates is that there may be other ways to manage this type of problem that can keep a project on track and preserve the relationship.

Lesson 1: Change Direction as Needed and Save Face

The Chinese philosopher Lao Tzu once stated, "If you do not change direction, you may end up where you are heading."[4] This was indeed the case with Aaron, who paid very close attention to what was happening and recognized an important change was needed. The restructuring, with a focus on incentivizing, helped to turn a situation that was not working into something productive for both parties.

Connected to this lesson was the need to save face. Fortunately, Aaron also recognized that dimension of the problem and brought in Lazo to address the lack of expertise Manufix had when it came to constructing the laser component of the project. Aaron understood the people at Manufix could not ask so, in effect, he asked for them. That action sufficed from a cultural point of view.

Lesson 2: When You Hit a Snag, Think to Restructure the Deal Before Walking Away

When CXX began to notice problems and saw that milestones were being missed, Aaron knew that something had to change. The first thought that came to his mind was to walk away and find another entity to do the work. However attractive that thought may have been, the change would be costly and time consuming. In this case, Aaron and his team resisted making that shift and, instead, restructured the deal in a way that would meet their underlying interests and needs. They did that by minimizing the up-front costs, back-end loading the contract, and creating incentives and ownership in the process on the part of Manufix.

In short, what CXX did matched the "can do" promises with a "can do" plan of action that worked for them and was acceptable to Manufix. As Aaron also shared, "It was critical to stay on top of them, by making frequent visits to China, and to make sure they knew we were there to protect our interests. We had a $100,000 learning experience we did not want to replicate."[5]

Lesson 3: Manage Your BATNA Effectively

Aaron and CXX's BATNA was to move on and find another company in China, or Taiwan, to complete the project. While that was certainly possible, the consequences in terms of time and money were significant. So even though there were alternatives for CXX, they were not nearly as attractive as they seemed at first blush.

Instead of exercising their BATNA, they used the concept to send a signal to Manufix that they could move on, but preferred to try to salvage the relationship by reworking it and adding another player to the equation that would make up for the deficiency. Manufix, which did not have a good BATNA, desperately wanted this project for numerous reasons, so they were disposed to accept what CXX was proposing.

Notes

1. Interview with David Lithwick.
2. Interview with David Lithwick.
3. Interview with David Lithwick.
4. Quote can be found here: http://beyondquarterlife.com/change-direction-may-end/
5. Interview with David Lithwick.

17

Going a Long Way to Make a Deal

Based on an interview with Howard Sheer

What do you do when you are a small company in one geographic location who is trying to do business and negotiate with a much larger entity half a world away? Then add in a clear power disparity to the mix – of which you are on the lesser end. Not an easy proposition to be confronted with.

However, while a power disparity existed in this particular negotiation, what if the other party never viewed the situation from that perspective or sought to use their clout? And if power was not the dominant frame in the negotiation, what was it that would speak to the other party and persuade them to ultimately do business with you? Finally, while we are at it, let's add in a strong dimension of cultural differences where respect and deference are fundamentally important.

As the previous paragraphs allude to, this negotiation was steeped in unusual dynamics and uncertainty. One party, based in the US, had limited but positive interactions and experiences with the other party based in India. With that experience in tow, the head of the US-based company decided he needed to travel all the way to India to show the other company how much he wanted their business. The negotiations, and the favorable outcome that unfolded from there, left both parties pleasantly surprised.

Background and the Negotiation Challenge

The company, called Ecru, is a small clothing company based in New York City. Ecru's CEO, Howard Sheer, led the negotiations with a potentially new supplier based in India, called Indego-pro. Sheer began looking to India as more and more unfavorable changes were taking place in China – where his previous supplier base existed.

Indegopro was a large factory group based primarily in India with facilities in other countries. Sheer very much wanted to work with Indegopro for a multitude of reasons, but he feared that they held all the cards in the negotiation and it would be a difficult process to meet his goals and make the deal profitable for the much smaller Ecru.

Sheer came to know about Indegopro through other textile mills he was working with on related projects. Sheer did his due diligence and investigated Indegopro thoroughly. As he did, he found that they served small entities similar to Ecru, but also big department stores like Gap and Banana Republic. He also found that Indegopro had a great track record of working with all of these different stores. Their quality, value, and public relations all checked out. Sheer's challenge was that Ecru was tiny in comparison. How would he persuade them that doing business with Ecru was worthwhile to them?

Preparing to Negotiate

As Sheer began to think about the upcoming negotiation he had amassed a bit of information to work from. Ecru had engaged

Indegopro on one order and Sheer was very happy with how they performed. The terms under which that first deal was done, however, were not at all ideal for Ecru. They were working under a Letter of Credit (LC), which they could manage, but LCs tend to be expensive and Ecru didn't have the ability to engage this way into the future. Put differently, Ecru needed the ability to finance the business and the bank would only open a limited number of LCs. Thus, Sheer knew the core of the negotiation was about a future partnership and the terms under which that arrangement would unfold. The precedent from the previous arrangement did not help his cause.

Sheer also knew that in Indian culture, having a strong relationship mattered a great deal when it came to doing business. Unfortunately, that was lacking. As he considered what to do given this reality, he knew that he needed to find a way to exhibit his seriousness and commitment to the relationship. Then it hit him. He would make a trip all the way to India to demonstrate his level of commitment.

Sheer knew that Indegopro had its original roots as a family business, but it had outgrown that. Indegopro was now a serious company with effective structures and professional management in place. They ran a very sophisticated operation and had significant contracts with many large and popular retailers.

As Sheer continued to think through his negotiation strategy, he remembered going to a negotiation training a few months prior and pulled out his materials to strategically prepare. Sheer concluded that it would be very important for him to try to control the agenda by framing the negotiation on his terms. To do that he would try to anchor the negotiations the way he wanted with a first offer and the terms that would be ideal to achieve. Of all the issues in the negotiation, the one that had the most value for him was moving away from an LC and to some favorable financing terms. LCs, in addition to what has been previously mentioned, cost money because the bank is charging interest on the letters. For Sheer, 90 days was his aspiration point or the best he could hope for, 60 days was his target, and 30 days was reservation point – anything below this point and the deal would not be acceptable.

The Negotiation

By going to India to meet in person, Sheer determined that he could be a bit bolder in his initial proposal. While he had not really met anyone in person, he believed his effort to travel a great distance gave him some leverage and bought him some goodwill. He understood that they had no idea who they were talking to, and maybe why they were even talking to him beyond the obvious. That stated, in addition to the things previously mentioned, another key for Sheer in the negotiation was to get Indegopro to ship the merchandise to customers and then pay them all in one order. The odds of doing a small amount of work, as Ecru had done, with a company like Indegopro and then asking them to extend credit was aspirational by any measure.

In going to India, Sheer was doing his best to bridge the cultural gap. He wanted to send a clear and unequivocal signal that he was very serious about working with Indegopro now and into the distant future. His goal was to get them to understand that he deeply valued their business, and he was prepared to invest in the relationship to prove it.

Sheer began the negotiation by taking a different tack and playing up the fact that he was not a giant retailer. He emphasized the small, boutique nature of Ecru and sought to use it to his advantage. However, he also wanted them to know that Ecru was an up-and-coming brand with plans to grow. To that end, he shared some specifics on Ecru's growth plan into the future. He encouraged Indegopro to get in on the upswing and used the principle of scarcity to do so.[1]

As the process unfolded, something, however, continued to gnaw at Sheer, and he wanted to probe the representatives of Indegopro about the issue. As he posed to his counterparts, "We are tiny compared to all these other operations – why do you want to work with us?"[2] The representatives of Indegopro said, in a very matter of fact manner, "We love your product, the quality level, and the unique design. We hope you will grow, and we want to be part of that."[3] As Sheer thought to himself, everyone has to have a smallest customer, so it might as well be Ecru.

After spending the day together and discussing things generally, Sheer turned to the specifics and the heart of the negotiation from his point of view. The primary issue was the financing terms. Sheer's opening offer was for 90-day terms based on receipt of goods, which in actuality was 120 days in payment terms because to ship the merchandise by boat would be 30 days in transit. To Sheer's surprise, the representatives at Indegopro had no issue with the 90 days. They countered with a proposed 1.75% flat finance charge, which for Sheer was considerably cheaper than opening an LC or tying up his credit line at the bank that he could use for other purposes.

Upon reflection, this was not an exceptionally challenging negotiation, but it was the unknowns of the negotiation parameters and the lack of a relationship that defined this situation. The representatives at Indegopro explained to Sheer after the agreement had been signed that they were very moved by the effort it took for him to come all the way to India and the professionalism of the presentation of his business plan for the future.

Lessons Learned

There are many ways to try to make a deal. Some of them require a lot more effort than others. However, sometimes that effort is well worth it and yields benefits that even exceed the investing party's aspirations.

Lesson 1: Showing Up

The primary lesson of this case is the importance of showing up and how critical that is for setting the tone of a negotiation. Many cultures around the world value face-to-face interactions and the importance of the relationship. Gestures, such as the one that Sheer took to travel to them and be respectful of their culture, went a long way to paving the path for the deal. In some respects, the details of this negotiation were not nearly as important as that act. Showing up in this manner demonstrated a commitment and a seriousness that companies value, along with the key element of veneration.

Sheer also connected with them personally, sharing a meal with them and meeting with a cross section of people in the company – from the CEO all the way down to some of the line workers.

Lesson 2: Power and Size Matter, but Not How You Think

On the surface of this negotiation Indegopro held all the cards from a power point of view. They were big, had a proven track record, and did not really need to do business with Ecru. However, neither Indegopro nor Sheer focused their energy or attention on that aspect of the negotiation. In fact, it was just the opposite. Sheer used Ecru's smaller size and unique product line to differentiate themselves and make them attractive to Indegopro.

Sheer also used the power of framing and anchoring to set up the negotiation the way he wanted. Sheer admitted that he did not know how Indegopro thought about the whole scenario, so he took a somewhat vague and general approach to the negotiation. He did this because he wanted to see what would evolve and also to make sure their standards were up to par for his company.

Ecru's size probably also helped in a different kind of way. Given the scope of Ecru's operation the risk was minimal to Indegopro. Furthermore, after the negotiation had ended in an agreement, Indegopro revealed that they were attracted to the deal because they saw Ecru's line being developed at the India facility.[4] Ecru could pay a bit more, and it was worth it to extend the credit to Ecru because they liked the product.

Lesson 3: Showing a Plan for Growth and the Art of What Could Be

In some regards one could argue that Ecru did not have a tremendous amount to offer Indegopro. However, upon further examination Ecru brought the promise of something bigger in the future and an opportunity for Indegopro to get in on the ground floor and grow with Ecru. In order to do this, Sheer had to exhibit to Indegopro what his plan was for the future and to get them to buy into it. His presentation to them at their facilities did just that and changed the conversation from a small firm and a limited deal to a small firm with significant upside and minimal risk.

Lesson 4: Uncertainty in Negotiation, First Offers, the Winner's Curse and Meeting Your Objectives

Every negotiation comes with uncertainty. While it is possible to feel out the parameters of a negotiation sometimes those edges are unknown, and it is unclear what is most important to the other side until the negotiation begins to unfold.

One general rule of thumb that exists in negotiation is that when you know and understand the parameters of a negotiation and the ZOPA it is best to make a first offer to frame and anchor a negotiation. However, when that is not the case and it is hard to obtain information about the negotiation scope and what the other wants, it is wisest to let the other party go first.

In this case, Sheer pushed a bit against that logic by making the first offer and using his aspiration point of 90 days. In the end he was able to obtain that in exchange for a small interest rate payment. As Sheer explained, "I didn't want to negotiate against myself, so I thought initially to ask for 60 days, but then went to 90 to make sure I was not undercutting myself. I was expecting them to push back a bit, but apparently that was not a key issue for them. I determined that I should just say – here is what I want – can you do it? If not, at least we would be starting from that anchor and not zero."[5]

While Sheer got what he wanted, this kind of outcome is often known as the winner's curse because he got what he asked for, but it is likely he could have had more.[6] Some might be disappointed by this, but Sheer was not because he met his objectives as he defined them. This is a very important point that many people miss when it comes to negotiation. If a negotiator defines their objectives clearly and thoughtfully, and meets them, then it does not matter what more you could have had.

Notes

1. In Cialdini's book *Influence: The Psychology of Persuasion*, he discusses six principles of persuasion and influence. One of the six ways in which he suggests people can be persuaded is through scarcity, which is the idea that people will miss out on something if they don't act quickly.
2. Interview with Howard Scheer.
3. Interview with Howard Scheer.
4. Part of Indegopro's goal was to keep the facilities full and running in India and Ecru's business helped contribute to that.
5. Interview with Howard Scheer.
6. The definition of the winner's curse is when you put an initial offer on the table and the other side immediately accepts it. The negotiator got what they wanted, but it is likely they could have had more.

18

Crossing Cultures and Crossing Wires

Based on an interview with Chang In Shin

We have already seen how a merger and acquisition negotiation can be quite difficult with a lot of pitfalls and challenges. Why stop there? Let's add another dimension to the equation, namely cultural constructs that are often hidden and silently guide negotiators' behaviors and approaches.

When negotiators consider culture, they often contemplate behaviors and customs, but as the reader will come to understand, that is just what can best be termed superficial culture. The more challenging aspects of culture from a negotiation point of view lie beneath the surface and are profoundly embedded in ways of acting, thinking, and believing. So, let's delve deeply to that level to understand what happened in this scenario.

Background and the Negotiation Challenge

This was a negotiation that took place in Pankyo, South Korea, regarding a merger and acquisition negotiation between a Korean biotechnology company and a German biotechnology company. Pankyo is an emerging digital city comparable to Silicon Valley in the United States. The South Korean government has been promoting Pankyo globally to attract foreign investors. Most of the high-tech ventures in South Korea are concentrated in the district called, aptly, Pankyo Techno Valley.

This particular negotiation occurred in a face-to-face capacity at the CEO's office of the Korean company, named Kyammi. The German company involved in the negotiation is called Bundascorp. Bundascorp's CEO visited South Korea for the series of negotiations in which Kyammi's CEO was seeking capital investment from Bundascorp. In return, Bundascorp's CEO was seeking to control the management of the Kyammi through a merger and eventual acquisition.

Preparing to Negotiate

The parties were not completely new to each other. They had maintained a somewhat distant business relationship for over 20 years. In this negotiation, Kyammi wanted to be an authorized subsidiary of Bundascorp and maintain its business relationship through their capital investment. They wanted this relationship because they would benefit from Bundascorp's excellent global reputation in the biotechnology field. Bundascorp wanted to control the management of Kyammi because they owned one of the leading biotechnologies in the world along with affluent human resources and regional networks that dominated the Asian market. Based on these positions, was it a good match that would benefit both companies?

On the one hand, the underlying interest of Kyammi was not to lose its majority stake in the company so they could still make their own decisions, while also maximizing the amount of investment from Bundascorp. On the other hand, Bundascorp wanted to take control of the Korean subsidiary company's shares in order to exploit the regional domination of Kyammi in Asia. By exercising its power over management, this task would be made much easier.

The Negotiation

While the negotiations had many dynamics, none were more critical to a solution than getting to the bottom of the cultural issue that underpinned each company's orientation and position. Kyammi's CEO perceived himself as the lower power party due to various cultural norms, although his company obtained the key technology that they needed to attract many foreign investors.

In the Korean cultural context, Korean parties seeking foreign investment perceive themselves as the lower power parties, given that their counterparts have financial capability and resources. Thus Korean companies in this position often abstain from speaking up in front of foreign parties whom they perceive as more powerful. As a result, Koreans engage in negotiation processes without communicating their needs and wants with the high-power parties.

Hofstede explains such phenomena as power distance, the extent to which different cultures perceive the notion of power.[1] As was previously mentioned, South Korea has the cultural tendency of not negotiating with parties whom they perceive to be more powerful. Such cultural tendencies force South Korean negotiators into a position where they do not engage in reciprocal negotiation processes, but rather they feel compelled to make "voluntary" concessions in advance of the actual negotiation.

As such, when the negotiation unfolded, cross-cultural differences in communicating their respective needs were clearly on display. Despite Kyammi's CEO experiencing significant discomfort with the way the Bundascorp's CEO negotiated, he did not express these emotions openly since such a demonstration would have been deeply frowned upon from a cultural point of view. This refrain by the Kyammi CEO was coupled with the Bundascorp CEO's direct and strongly assertive approach advocating for his company's needs. The contrast could not have been starker.

Another cultural factor involved was the age of the negotiators. In a South Korean cultural context, more senior people are supposed to get resources first and then distribute them based on the loyalty demonstrated by more junior employees. In the case of Kyammi, the CEO was much younger than the Bundascorp's CEO, and this was another reason why he perceived himself as a lower power party and acted as such.

The last cultural factor that was prevalent from a South Korean point of view was the value of harmony. This value emanated from a combination of Buddhism and Taoism belief systems. Koreans value social harmony more than virtually any other factor and, as such, openly disagreeing in social interactions is simply not done.[2] Furthermore, and connecting back to the previous point, disagreeing with seniors or elders usually results in retaliation – both personally and professionally – and culminates in a disadvantage from a resource allocation perspective.

The negotiation process progressed simply because Kyammi's CEO made begrudging concession after concession. He did so for the aforementioned reasons and because of the critical importance of maintaining a harmonious relationship above all else. As a result, Kyammi's CEO lost most of his company shares through these voluntary concessions, allowing Bundascorp to take over 65% of the company.

In this negotiation situation, an agreement was reached mainly with the unilateral concessions of Kyammi's CEO. In the end the parties agreed to split the shares to 65:35, with Bundas-corp's CEO controlling the management over the Asian market. However, no creative solution was achieved due to both parties' different cultural expectations. Kyammi's CEO did not want to say no to his German counterpart due to the fear of losing the long-term relationship and breaking the Korean cultural code of harmony. Put another way, South Koreans would rather reach an agreement than to try to openly resolve clear conflicts of interests that would disrupt basic levels of goodwill.

This was not, however, where the negotiation ended. When South Koreans engage in this kind of behavior, they frequently do not comply with the agreement they signed. In order to comply and implement an agreement they need to be satisfied with the negotiation process itself as well as the personal relationship with their counterpart(s). So all of the voluntary concessions made by Kyammi did not mean they would comply with the agreement during the implementation phase.

When making these voluntary concessions, South Korean companies expect that their unilateral actions will bring about a constructive business relationship based on mutual trust and loyalty. From their perspective, they have demonstrated their loyalty to the high-power party and that should eventually benefit them as well. If that reciprocal bond does not evolve, the overall business relationship will break down.

Relational satisfaction is a critical issue to South Korean negotiators. They believe that all successful business negotiations in South Korea should be based on the personal satisfaction of a business relationship. Under the cultural ideology of Confucianism, most Asian negotiators tend to harmonize with the demands of their counterparts by making voluntary concession, trusting that such concession will bring about the compatible demonstration of loyalty and exclusive business relationship by their counterparts.

The outcome of this negotiation was far from optimal – particularly for Kyammi, but also for Bundascorp. By making their concessions, as their culture dictated, Kyammi attempted to put itself into a new and different relationship with Bundascorp. Bundascorp unfortunately did not understand that was what was happening and, as a result, took advantage of the situation and the relationship. Interestingly however, due to the very strong emphasis on the relationship by the CEO of Kyammi, the business relationship has persisted and, while not balanced, it continues to this day. One can only imagine how much more fruitful the relationship would be if the situation had properly met Kyammi's cultural expectations.

Lessons Learned

There are a number of lessons that are key for people to understand who are negotiating in an international cultural context such as this. As the reader can envision, the dilemma herein required a very attuned negotiator to all the potential cultural nuances involved.

Lesson 1: The Spoken and Unspoken Elements of Culture

First, culture greatly influences the way people negotiate and communicate their needs. Culture not only controls the ways in which people raise (or do not raise) issues, but also their ability to openly resolve any disputes or conflicts that might arise during the process. Furthermore, even discussing this lack of an ability to deal with conflict in an overt manner is frowned upon, rendering it a minefield if one is unaware of these cultural foundations.

The key to dealing with all of this is understanding the culture one will be interacting with and their ways of living, working, and negotiating. Of course, when learning about a culture, people tend to initially learn about the general tenets. This is a good starting point, but has to be coupled with a knowledge that there are also important differences within a culture. For example, regional differences within a culture can be profound and are also quite important to be cognizant of and to manage accordingly.

Lesson 2: Process Matters

Second, process matters greatly in negotiation, and how people conduct themselves during a negotiation can send signals and carry various connotations. In this case, a little brother–big brother process was put in place by the Kyammi CEO based largely on South Korean cultural expectations influenced by age and the nature of the relationship between juniors and seniors. With that type of dependent process came a series of hidden expectations that shaped the negotiation and created confusion and unspoken frustrations that manifested in a suboptimal agreement and an unbalanced relationship.

Lesson 3: Hidden Expectations Wreak Havoc on Negotiation

Third, the process choices led Kyammi's CEO to make certain assumptions about their expectations toward the Bundascorp's CEO. Kyammi's CEO believed the Bundascorp's CEO would naturally understand the type of relationship that was evolving and honor what was taking shape. He assumed it would be common knowledge that if a less powerful party goes into a negotiation with a more powerful party and starts making concessions that, in return, they will be taken care of by the more powerful party. If that does not happen, the more powerful party's needs will be met in the short term, but not in the longer term and the relationship will likely collapse as a result of these misaligned expectations.

Lesson 4: The Importance of Pre-negotiation and Negotiating the Negotiation

Fourth, the example of Kyammi and Bundascorp teaches us the importance of pre-negotiation and negotiating the negotiation with Asian counterparts. Due to the different expectations about what negotiation means, South Koreans tend to build personal relationships first prior to the actual business negotiations.[3] So the best chance for a successful negotiation with an Asian counterpart starts with a pre-negotiation process to negotiate the different expectations and gain alignment on many underlying aspects of the process.

Notes

1. Hofstede, G. *Culture's Consequences* (Beverley Hills, CA: Sage Publication, 1980).
2. Incidentally, this is important not just for South Koreans, but for many other East Asian countries as well.
3. This is also true for other countries in Asia such as Japan and China.

Government and Daily Life Cases

A tremendous number of negotiations happen all around us every day – whether it is between civil society entities, hostage situations, or at the governmental level between warring factions. Akin to the business cases that have been previously presented, these cases cover a vast array of areas. What is interesting is the similarities involved despite the disparate nature of the examples.

From a governmental point of view, whether it is within governments, between agencies, or between governments and opposition groups, negotiation is used to solve budget problems, interagency disputes, or charting a new course between parties that have been fighting for decades. That stated, governmental negotiations can be distinct from other types of negotiation processes due to a number of factors – including the number of actors involved, the varied constituencies they serve, and the bureaucracy they must manage.

The first case in this section has to do with a very unique situation between a United Nations entity and a sovereign government over the holding of hostages. Through a serendipitous series of events, along with thorough follow-through by the people involved, a situation involving refugees was resolved effectively. The negotiation required walking a very fine line between freeing the refugees without blaming the government and the captors involved. Furthermore, having a deep understanding of the cultural norms that underpinned the negotiation process was essential to success.

The second case also occurred at the governmental level, but this time it was part of a negotiation during the peace process in Colombia. While the parties had made extraordinary progress, the process faced a crisis. A stalemate arose around the proposed language for dealing with transitional justice issues. One of the negotiators, who happened to be a former general, had seen previous processes lay blame for past atrocities squarely at the feet of the military while he felt there were many other actors that should also be held accountable. That is where things got bogged down. How they dealt with that delicate issue was surprising.

The third governmental case was also in the context of a peace process – this time in the Philippines. A deal for a key part of the overall peace process had been secured and the parties, along with the facilitators, were en route by plane for the formal signing. During the flight, however, one of the party's governments nixed the agreement. The parties and the facilitation team had to work quickly to keep the situation from devolving back into violence. By working tirelessly and having previously thought through alternate plans, all involved were able to pull the pieces back together and salvage the negotiation process.

The fourth case shifts gears back to North America and a crisis negotiation in Calgary, Alberta, Canada.[1] In this example, a crisis negotiator with the Calgary Police engaged with a man who was struggling after a significant change occurred with his wife. The negotiation took some unique twists and turns, culminating in an unexpected outcome.

The fifth case occurred in the United States and involved negotiating for the freeing of hostages and the apprehension of an individual who held very strong anti-government sentiments. The hostage taker was threatening violence to those around him and the surrounding community. Through the delicate work of the hostage negotiation team, supported by the police, the hostage taker gave himself up and the situation was peaceably resolved. This effort required significant coordination between many state and local officials as well as an understanding of what was really motivating the hostage taker.

The sixth case was another hostage negotiation scenario in the United States. This negotiation perfectly demonstrated a model that the Federal Bureau of Investigation (FBI) has been using for many years to build rapport between the hostage negotiator and the hostage taker. As a result of that rapport, all the hostages were freed without harm, the hostage taker peaceably gave himself up, and the hostage negotiator was able to understand a critical aspect of what was motivating the hostage taker.

The seventh example was a difficult negotiation between two nonprofit organizations. Both organizations were doing important and meaningful work in the world. However, they had a problem. The names of the two organizations were very similar, creating confusion between supporters and donors alike. The two sides worked amicably for quite some time to try to negotiate a solution, but to no avail. Eventually they sought the help of a mediator. After listening to the sides and contemplating the conundrum, the mediator asked a simple counterintuitive question that unlocked the key to a solution.

The eighth and final scenario in this section was a contract negotiation between a professor and a university. What made this case unique was that the professor was based in one country and was asked to teach at a university in another country. The case proved to be a very useful example of the framing of a negotiation and how relationship building over time became the key to finding what each truly valued – thereby creating a better deal for all involved.

Note

1. For a useful analysis on the difference between a crisis negotiation and a hostage negotiation, please see https://leb.fbi.gov/articles/featured-articles/crisis-or-hostage-negotiation-the-distinction-between-two-important-terms

19

"It All Began with a Crumpled-Up Note"

Based on an interview with Karen Hanrahan

High-stakes negotiations take many forms, but there is no higher stake than when human lives hang in the balance. When negotiating where people's lives are in question, the pressure and the consequences negotiators feel are often beyond words. The stress of the situation can lead to dynamics that encourage tough talk and demands. Two common outcomes follow when this strong-arm approach is taken – either the other side acquiesces to a demand or the process degenerates into stalemate and failure.

This type of negotiation challenge is complicated further when different cultural norms are added to the equation. Cultures vary greatly when it comes to negotiation and what is, and is not, appropriate. In many places around the world a key cultural concept is face saving – or the preservation of one's reputation – at all cost. In fact, a negotiated deal in these cultures cannot be consummated unless face saving underlines the agreement for all sides involved.

This fragile mix was on display in the case that follows. The lives of a group of girls and women were at issue. An international team had to negotiate for their release. A governmental entity had to grant permission for the negotiations. Those on the ground – both captors and captees – had to be given a way out that enabled them to save face. Here is how this complex story unfolded.

Background and the Negotiation Challenge

"A man handed me a handwritten note on a crumpled piece of paper" recounted Karen, who worked for the United Nations High Commissioner for Refugees (UNHCR) as a senior protections officer in the Western province of Herat in Afghanistan focusing on assisting refugees and internally displaced persons (IDPs).[1] This is the cryptic way in which the negotiation started; the year was 2002.

One day Karen was conducting a human rights training in one of the villages that was run by a former warlord. She received the aforementioned note from an anonymous person in the kitchen of the Foreign Ministry's local office while they were having lunch. The enigmatic note implored her to look into a situation in a nearby village. The note alluded to the fact that there were a group of girls and women that were being held against their will. The note, which was given to her assistant and translator, laid out the problem and the issue to a small degree.

Based on this lead and needing to understand the full extent of the story, Karen and her team began to look into the situation further. After tracking down the informant, he explained that he knew about this situation because he had been giving these women food and trying to help them. Of course, at first, he was very reluctant to talk for fear of retribution. If the government found out who was sharing this information it was likely that he would have been imprisoned or killed.

Karen and her team did further investigations to determine if there was any substance to the claim. However, this had to be done very delicately given that the whole process was steeped in cross-cultural issues. Admittedly, it took a while (approximately a month) to get details from this person and other sources. The process of building a relationship with the informant was critical so that they knew they could trust Karen and her team, but also so Karen and her team could trust him and the information he was giving them. It was a very serious claim to accuse a governmental entity of such a crime, so they needed to be as certain as they could before taking any action.

The informant explained that the people being held were Iranian refugees. However, getting that precise information was difficult because culturally Afghanis speak in a nonlinear fashion. As such, Karen and colleagues had to piece a lot of the story together. They also had to engage in efforts to triangulate what they were learning so they were certain they were correct.[2] The team reached a point where they did not have all the information they needed, but felt there were enough solid leads to suggest that these girls and women were indeed being held in the place that was described. They also learned there were 22 girls and women being held whose ages ranged from 10 to mid-20s.

Now that they were fairly confident the women were being held against their will, and that they were being used for inappropriate activities, Karen had to think about what to do next. In Afghani culture these women could not simply be released on their own or they would likely be killed. Women who are alone in this manner could be stoned or killed just for being without a male relative. Even if there were only rumors of such a situation, that might be enough to create a dangerous scenario for the girls and women.

Eventually Karen and her colleagues determined that they needed to take the first step in addressing the issue. After some back and forth deliberations, they determined their best initial course of action was to write a letter to the local representative of the Ministry of Foreign Affairs laying forth the problem as they had come to understand it. They would then see what the response was and take the situation forward from there. That was really all they could do at this juncture.

Preparing to Negotiate

The choice by Karen and her colleagues to write an official letter, instead of taking a more informal approach, was an important one that they debated for quite some time. They had made unofficial inquiries on the ground to try to resolve the issue, but the typical response was, "That situation is not possible. It would never happen here."[3] In short, the informal route was a dead end, shrouded in secrecy. Going the official route was a strategic decision, and one they ultimately realized was the only real way to address the problem.

Karen and her colleagues did not know anyone in the Ministry of Foreign Affairs in the Western provinces. Sending the letter was certainly risky because it could get leaked to other sources. Adding to that challenge was the fact that once a letter like this was written to people at the official level it would have to be answered. The one thing Karen was pretty certain about was that if the person in the Foreign Ministry in the Western Provinces did not respond, this would be sent on to the Foreign Ministry in the capital, Kabul. A responsible person at that level would have to provide some type of answer.

The team took some time to craft a very carefully worded and respectful letter. They explained that they had learned there were 22 girls and women in the custody of the Foreign Ministry who might need help. They explained further that these girls and women were refugees, and under international law, UNHCR must assist them and was mandated to do so. As such, they needed access to them to understand exactly what was going on.

The contact at the Foreign Ministry for the Western Provinces replied, which lead to a series of back and forth exchanges. Initially they claimed nothing like what was in the letter was happening in their province. They shared that they have refugees from Iran who go back and forth across the border all the time. As they asserted, "This was probably just one of those episodes."[4] They tried to brush it off, but to no avail.

The Negotiation

Karen and her colleagues were finally able to get a series of in-person meetings. The initial goal was to get the Foreign Ministry officials to recognize that this situation was indeed happening. They ultimately acknowledged this to a degree, but it took multiple meetings and a lot of careful framing and nudging. It became clear during the negotiations that the Ministry officials wanted to be heard and for the United Nations (UN) team to accept the narrative that the Ministry was protecting the women from forces outside that might kill them should they be freed. Rightly or wrongly, that framing was needed to get access.

It turned out that the notion of face saving, which is a critical Afghani cultural construct, underpinned the entire negotiation process. The UN team had to find a way to acknowledge that the Foreign Ministry was doing the right thing, but that the girls and women needed to be released into their custody. Unlike many human rights approaches that focus on calling these issues out publicly, the key was "not to directly accuse the people involved or the negotiation would have been over before it ever started."[5]

Fortunately for Karen and her team, they had adopted a problem-solving mindset. Without that way of thinking and overall approach, an agreement would not have been possible.

Karen asked the Ministry officials, "How can I get access to them and then how can we help them?"[6] Admittedly this was a fine line to walk. However, through persistence, eventually the Foreign Ministry conceded something was amiss and granted them the permission they were seeking. This opened the door to the next phase of the process.

In addition to the non-accusatory approach, the team also used their role and status as UNHCR representatives as a reason for them to be involved. As they explained to the Foreign Ministry officials, "These women are refugees. It is our job, confirmed by international law, to assist and take care of them. We just want access to them so we can talk to them and make sure they are okay."[7] It also helped that Afghanistan was a member of the UN and accepted their presence. If the team had been representing a government, they likely would not have been granted an entrée.

When the Foreign Ministry did allow them to meet with the girls and women, they explained the parameters clearly: "You can just interview them and make sure you understand we are trying to protect them."[8] Karen and her translator alone went to meet with the girls and women in a remote compound run by the Foreign Ministry. They were able to confirm there were indeed 22 girls and women in the compound. They began by talking to them about what happened in Iran and how they got to this place.

With these nascent conversations, an entirely new negotiation began with the girls and women. It took months to build rapport with the girls and women and to get them to share what was really going on. Having open conversations in the compound and sharing information was difficult in normal circumstances, let alone in the open air with guards nearby.

The negotiations were not easy and led to a lot of challenges. Tragically two of the women killed themselves over the course of the negotiations. The trauma they had experienced was simply too great. As the remainder of the women slowly revealed they were being sexually abused, the onus fell squarely on Karen and her team to figure out how to get them out.

One critical element to the negotiations, according to Karen, was to continue to show up. At the same time, they had to show the Ministry officials that what they were doing would not lead to serious consequences for them. After all, as they shared with the Foreign Ministry counterparts, "we are just chatting." There were, however, places where they did have to take a stand. For example, the guards around the compound were making the girls and women nervous and preventing them from speaking freely. Karen insisted that the guards be removed, and the Foreign Ministry acquiesced.

The entire process, from the first time Karen and her interpreter met with the women, lasted approximately six months. In the beginning the girls and women would not say much. Showing up over and over again, listening, and learning about them was critical to get them to slowly open up. There was so much shame that eventually came out with regard to what had happened to them. It was deeply painful for the women to discuss, and even harder with the cultural taboos that existed in that part of the world related to sexuality.

As the negotiations inched forward with the girls and women, it slowly became clear that the Foreign Ministry recognized this as a problem and saw Karen and her team as the way out. It helped that the team framed the situation as a problem to be solved and the framing of "let us help you solve it" became paramount.

The negotiations with the girls and women was happening in parallel to the continued negotiation with the Foreign Ministry. The team was very clear with the Foreign Ministry that they were paying attention, a spotlight was on the issue, and they were not going away until this was resolved.

The team had succeeded in getting access and were moving toward a solution on freeing them when another conundrum emerged. The girls and women could not just be released. The team also had to look for a longer-term solution for them. While a few wanted to go back to their families in Iran, many did not have families to go back to or wanted to move on. After some extensive searching, Karen and colleagues found a women's home in Kabul. The goal became to get them to that home or back to Iran.

Eventually Karen and her interpreter wrapped up the official interviews and made a series of recommendations to the Ministry. This came after they tried to engage the Ministry in a process of option generation, but the Ministry seemed to prefer to defer to them on the solution. In the end the team was able to get the girls and women released, emphasizing the notion that the Ministry clearly cared about their well-being, and the Ministry came out looking good in the process. Some of the women went back to Iran, and the rest to the aforementioned women's home in Kabul.

Lessons Learned

This case is extremely rich with lessons due to the complex nature of the negotiation, the cultural aspects that underlay it, and the fine line the negotiators needed to walk metaphorically.

Lesson 1: Face Saving and Taking a Joint Problem-Solving Approach

The key to this entire negotiation was the concept of face saving and how the UNHCR team understood that and respected it. They had to tread very carefully between helping the Foreign Ministry save face while also achieving their objective of getting the women freed. A face-saving solution, however, would not have been possible without a problem-solving mindset and approach. In order to find this delicate balance, the team had to stay focused on their goal of getting the women released. This required thinking like the Foreign Ministry and crafting solutions that would also meet their interests – particularly the need to come out looking like a protector.

Lesson 2: The Importance of Planning Instead of Having a Concrete Plan

In a negotiation such as this it was virtually impossible to have a plan. After Karen received the initial handwritten note and verified its veracity, she knew her goal needed to be to get the girls and women free. However, how to do that was a completely different challenge and initially unclear. The process needed to be iterative.

Some planning, such as understanding the cultural issues involved, could be done, but much had to be sorted out slowly along the way. This approach also was a result of working with incomplete information and connecting things together one puzzle piece at a time.

Lesson 3: Relationship Building, Trust, and Showing Up Time and Again

Another critical element of this negotiation was taking the time to slowly build the relationships needed to solve this conundrum. In Afghani culture one cannot trust the other until they know them well. This was the case with the informant in the kitchen, but also the people in the Foreign Ministry. The principle of developing relationships as a first step in negotiation cuts across all spectrums.

Related to the notion of relationship building was the importance of showing up time and again. Karen and her interpreter spent many months going back and forth to the remote compound in order to send the signal to the Foreign Ministry and, more importantly, to the girls and women that they were serious and they were not leaving until they had freed them.

Lesson 4: Knowing When to Advocate and Blow the Whistle versus When to Negotiate

When it comes to human rights issues the common approach is advocacy – to shout from the rooftops, shine a light on the problem, and to put pressure on the perpetrators. In this case, the team made the opposite decision – to negotiate. Why? As Karen explained, "It is important to blow the whistle when you are far away, but negotiation is more appropriate when you are on the ground, lives are at stake, and you can do something about it."[9] In short, which approach to use has to be determined on a case-by-case basis considering the unique dynamics involved.

In reality there is often a mix of the two. Even in this situation, we saw times when Karen and her colleagues put some pressure on the Foreign Ministry. When they did apply pressure, they could revert back to negotiation as a way of also showing the Foreign Ministry a way out of the conundrum.

Lesson 5: Managing Multiple Negotiations and Sequencing Them Properly

The last lesson from this case is the problem of managing multiple negotiations all at once and sequencing them properly. From the negotiation with the informant in the kitchen, to the back and forth with the Ministry of Foreign Affairs, and on to the negotiation with the girls and women, there were a lot of negotiation streams crossing. However, while these were different processes, they were not completely independent of one another. The progress with the girls and women cleared up some challenges in the negotiation with the Foreign Ministry and vice versa. Furthermore, the sequencing of the issues, and who should talk to whom at any given moment, required strategic thinking and planning.

Notes

1. An internally displaced person is someone from a particularly country who has had to flee their homes to another part of the country but does not leave the country.
2. In this context, triangulate means getting the same information from a number of different sources to make certain it was true.
3. Interview with Karen Hanrahan.
4. Interview with Karen Hanrahan.
5. In other instances, she had taken a much more direct approach and accused people of violating human rights.
6. Interview with Karen Hanrahan.
7. Interview with Karen Hanrahan.
8. At one point during the negotiations, the Ministry said the women were criminals. Some had indeed been jailed in Iran for being out of their home without a man with them. However, this was really tangential to the overall story.
9. Interview with Karen Hanrahan.

20

The Difference between Stalemate and Solution? A Different Word

Based on an interview with William Ury

Many decades-long conflicts have numerous difficulties to them, including hardened positions, significant distrust between the parties, and deep physical and psychological wounds that have been opened from many years of fighting. As such, bringing about peace within these deeply divided places requires exceedingly delicate negotiation approaches, techniques, and tactics. Equally important, these negotiations necessitate a very creative mindset amidst strong forces pushing in the direction of continued conflict and war. The conflict in Colombia was a classic example of all of these dimensions and was the longest-running conflict in the Americas, stretching from the mid-1960s until 2016 when an elusive agreement was reached. Pundits gave the process little chance for success, but an agreement was indeed consummated, and the process has continued to evolve to this day.[1]

Peace processes have many defining moments, big and small, that propel the process forward and create critical momentum. One such moment in the Colombian peace process happened in 2016 when a popular well-respected general threatened to permanently pull out of the process – undermining critical support from the domestic audience and the military sector. Through some outside help, simple questions, creative thinking, and selective word choice the negotiators involved were able to solve the issue and rescue the process and all the progress that had been made to date. Consider how those involved accomplished this feat.

Background and the Negotiation Challenge

Most societal conflicts are very complicated, including numerous parties and many varied dynamics impacting the situation. Colombia fit that category perfectly with numerous internal divides as well as regional influences and international involvement. Broadly speaking, the conflict was between the government and two Marxist rebel groups – the Revolutionary Armed Forces of Colombia (FARC) and the smaller National Liberation Army (ELN). The toll of the conflict – which began in the 1960s and stretched for over 54 years – was devastating. According to the Council on Foreign Relations, 220,000 people died, 25,000 disappeared, and 5.7 million were internally displaced.[2]

The conflict was very much about ideology, but also about political power. The FARC and ELN emerged in the 1960s after a decade of political violence that ensued between 1948 and 1958. These two groups were excluded from a power-sharing agreement that ended the violence. The FARC was composed of militant communists and peasant self-defense groups, while the smaller ELN was dominated by students, Catholic radicals, and left-wing intellectuals who hoped to replicate Fidel Castro's communist revolution.[3] The FARC and ELN opposed the privatization of natural resources and believed they represented the poor against a corrupt government dominated by the wealthy.

Over the years the FARC used kidnapping, extortion, and drug trafficking to keep their struggle alive. In the early 2000s it is estimated that the FARC supplied the world with almost 90% of its cocaine. Other right-wing groups got involved in the trafficking, thereby setting up more violence and a fractionating of the parties. This led to widespread killing and chaos. The ELN also took part in kidnapping and extortion, but initially did not get involved in drug trafficking. Eventually, out of financial necessity, they also began to traffic in cocaine.

Then, in the 2002 presidential election, Álvaro Uribe was elected on a platform that pledged to take a hard line against the FARC and ELN guerrillas. As the Council on Foreign Relations reported, "As his administration cracked down on the leftist rebel groups, violence fell dramatically: homicides fell by 40 percent and kidnappings by 80 percent during Uribe's first term, but international rights groups accused Uribe's administration of violating human rights. . . . Many experts say that the Uribe administration's crackdown laid the foundation for peace talks. By the time the FARC agreed to negotiations, in 2012, its ranks had fallen to some seven thousand members."[4]

In 2010 Juan Manuel Santos was elected president after having served as Defense Minister in Uribe's administration. Santos began to put out feelers to the FARC about a negotiated solution to the conflict.[5] At the same time, he created an international team of negotiation advisors to prepare and assist him and his negotiating team. The team was an unlikely combination, including Jonathan Powell, former chief of staff to British Prime Minister for Tony Blair and chief negotiator for the Northern Ireland conflict; Shlomo Ben Ami, a former Israeli foreign minister, and a veteran of the Oslo Peace Process; Joaquin Villalobos, former commander of the FMLN (El Salvador guerrillas); and William Ury of the Harvard Negotiation Project, co-author of the best-selling negotiation book *Getting to Yes*. These advisors worked closely with Santos and his team for seven years throughout the peace process, making over twenty-five trips to Colombia.[6]

Preparing to Negotiate

The negotiation process began by discussing the issue of agrarian reform and conditions for political participation of all players and made some surprising strides forward. The biggest sticking point was the cessation of hostilities between the government and the FARC and ultimately what would happen to the FARC if they were to lay down their weapons and agree to integrate back into Colombian society. This issue related directly to the problem of transitional justice, typical in these kinds of conflicts.

Transitional justice and the reintegration of opposition forces have proven very difficult in many other conflicts.[7] The dilemma is that, when a peace agreement is signed, the armed forces on each side often receive the bulk of the blame for the conflict, are held most accountable, and are given the stiffest penalties. While this is understandable in many ways, other entities – governmental and nongovernmental – who were deeply involved in the decision-making process often move into the future with impunity.[8] The ultimate question with regard to this problem is how do societies move forward while also dealing with the past and healing the wounds inflicted by the conflict?

In Colombia this issue was no different in terms of importance and difficulty. At one point, the negotiations over transitional justice broke down for a month. President Santos reached out to Ury and asked for his help. Ury packed his bags.

The stalemate came from one of the key government negotiators who was a retired general and who had previously served
as the head of the Colombian Armed Forces. The general vehemently opposed the government's transitional justice proposal.
He had studied past truth commissions, in conflicts such as El
Salvador, and had concluded that the agreements always ended
up blaming the military in a disproportionate manner. The general demanded that the proposal be withdrawn, and another
approach be taken to deal with the issue. The other negotiators
tried desperately for weeks to persuade him of the proposal's
merits, but the general would not budge.

The general felt so strongly about the issue that he withdrew from the negotiations in Havana, Cuba, where the talks
were being held, in a manner that became public instantly. News
of the general's withdrawal spread through the media with a
lot of support expressed for the general due to his popularity.
This was no ordinary stalemate. Without the active support of
the military, an agreement might simply not be reached or have
much of a chance of surviving into the future. The negotiations
were practically frozen while the president sought to find a solution that would persuade the general to return to Havana for the
talks. A full month elapsed without any progress.

This is what Ury knew as he left for Bogota. He understood
generally what the problem was, but did not know what underpinned the general's perspective. This would take some digging
that would require a lot of careful listening.

The Negotiation

Shortly after Ury arrived, he met with the general one to one
and began by asking him, "What is your real concern?" The general shared his worry about the military getting blamed in different peace processes, and he was not willing to have that happen

in Colombia. As the general shared, "The language specifies the collective responsibility of institutional actors – and I know 'institutional actors' is just a code name for the army."[9]

After that meeting Ury met with the other members of the government's delegation to listen to them. The strongest voice was that of the former vice president, who was leading the negotiations. He explained the importance of this aspect of the agreement: "We absolutely have to include the language around collective responsibility. We cannot stand in front of the world and say that we are not in any way collectively responsible for all the tragic events that have happened in this country. It would make us a laughingstock of the world. We need that language in there." The team remained divided and many members were frustrated and angry; some of them also threatened to resign. The peace commissioner believed his job was on the line.

Ury then decided to ask the full delegation to come together to unpack the issue. When they were all together, Ury began, "Let me just understand what the real problem is here. Let's put the problematic language up on the whiteboard." The draft text read, "assigning collective responsibility to Institutional actors and guerrilla groups." So Ury then asked the general, "So, what is the problem with this language?" The general explained for all to hear, "Well, the problem is that, we all know, the word 'Institutional' means the army."

Ury decided to dig further into the language specifically. "Okay. How can we rephrase this in some way that it doesn't point right at the army? What if, for example, we replace the word 'Institutional' with the word 'State' so it is clear that it is the whole government that is collectively responsible?" The general asked, "Do we need the word 'collective'?" The others explained that particular word was important because it was not merely individuals who had committed human rights violations, but collective entities with joint responsibility.

Ury tried again after the previous explanation. "So, if we just change that word 'Institutional' to 'State' will that be acceptable?" The general paused and reflected for a moment and finally said, "I guess it is okay. After all, the word 'State' does not single out the army but includes all the decision makers and governmental actors involved." Ury asked the others if this phrasing was suitable for them. One by one, they all agreed. As Ury recounted, "Everyone looked around in shock when they realized the problem had been solved – in twenty minutes."[10]

The group left and went to the president's office and shared the news. The president approved the language and the negotiators flew back to Havana to resume the negotiations.[11] With this obstacle removed, the two parties went on to negotiate long and hard on other issues and eventually reached an agreement on the thorny issue of transitional justice.

Lessons Learned

Stalemates in negotiation happen for many reasons and persist primarily due to a positional back and forth. When parties are in the throes of such a period in negotiation, the challenges seem almost insurmountable. That is when a shift or change is needed to break the deadlock and get the process moving again.

Lesson 1: Getting Locked into Positions Happens to the Best of Us

First, this is a classic case of getting locked into positions. The general had a position that the military was not going to be the only entity to be blamed for the crimes and atrocities that had transpired. After all, he had seen that happen in the past and he did not believe it was an unreasonable position to take. However, instead of thinking about different ways that the issue could be framed or addressed he became locked into that singular notion. When he received pushback from other members of the negotiating team – who were also taking a positional approach – he dug in and ultimately withdrew from the talks before being drawn back in.

The way out, as Ury exhibited, was through some simple and straightforward questions that uncovered the underlying interests involved. Once those were unearthed some potential solutions rose to the surface that worked for all involved.

Lesson 2: Language Matters – a Lot

Second, negotiators are often very focused on *what* they want, but not nearly enough on *how* they want to say something. In this case the "how" was critically important. The changing of one word – from "Institutional" to "State" – made all the difference. It was not, of course, simply a different word choice, but also what that word conveyed. Sometimes delving into the language people use is the key to reframing a situation that is stuck.

The change in language had the added effect of moving the conversation from positions to interests. On the one hand, the word "Institutions" carried a certain connotation for the general. The implication of this word was unacceptable because of the concern related to singular blame. "State," on the other hand, was a more encompassing term from the general's perspective and more accurately reflected the shared sense of responsibility that lay at the heart of the issue for him.

Lesson 3: The Challenge of Transference and the Assumptions It Brings

Finally, the concept of transference is a challenge that sometimes plagues negotiations. According to Fukushima, transference is "The (transferring) of old patterns to new situations that organizes and gives meaning to present circumstances."[12] Put differently, people are prone to apply previous experiences to new situations that are similar. This was the case with the general. While he had not directly been involved in other negotiations where blame was heaped solely on the military, he had read how previous negotiations to deal with the past had reached this conclusion. He did not want that to happen in Colombia. Whether it would have been the same or not is hard to know, but it was clearly an assumption he was making and a chance he was not willing to take. The transference of these lessons absolutely impacted his thinking and shaped his approach to the negotiation.

Notes

1. The peace agreement is in a very tenuous state as of this writing. After Santos left office, the new president, Ivan Duque, has taken a hard line toward the FARC and not pursued peace in the manner that Santos did.
2. Felter, C., and D. Renwick, "Colombia's Civil Conflict," Council on Foreign Relations, January 11, 2017, https://www.cfr.org/backgrounder/colombias-civil-conflict
3. Ibid.
4. Ibid.
5. Ibid.
6. It should be noted that the ELN were not part of the peace agreement.
7. According to the Peace Building Initiative, transitional justice is defined as helping to prevent the recurrence of violent conflict and foster sustainable peace by establishing a historical record and countering denial; ensuring accountability and ending impunity; and fostering reconciliation and socio-political reconstruction. See http://www.peacebuildinginitiative.org/indexf0e6.html?pageId=1883
8. There are notable exceptions to this, such as Slobodan Milošević from the former Yugoslavia, but the general statement holds true.
9. Interview with William Ury.
10. Quotations are from an interview with William Ury and from a speech he gave to the Scottish Parliament on May 12, 2018, entitled, "Common Good Politics: A New Enlightenment: How Mediators Can Lead the Way."
11. The negotiations were being held in Havana, Cuba. It is not uncommon for negotiations to address a civil war be held in another country so the parties feel some freedom and more at ease.
12. Fukushima, S. "What you bring to the table. Transference and Countertransference in the Negotiation Process," *Negotiation Journal* 15(2): 169–80.

21

Adaptability in the Face of Uncertainty: Saving the Philippines Peace Process after a Last-Minute Reversal

Based on an interview with David Gorman

Some complex negotiations are akin to putting together a puzzle, but without a clear idea of what the completed puzzle will ultimately look like. In these scenarios, negotiators and third parties have to work with the pieces in front of them, to try to see how they fit together, and gradually move inwards from a broad framework to placing the last, and most difficult pieces, into place.

There may be no more difficult negotiation than trying to end a large-scale societal conflict. Due to the sheer number of parties involved, the issues in question, and the forces that may be benefitting from a conflict, the odds are definitively against finding a solution. However, there are always exceptions, and they must be studied for how they achieved success. Consider the example below from the Philippines. This process was complicated and required some adaptive thinking when a last-minute reversal threw the entire process into doubt. Fortunately, due to the efforts of a facilitator and larger contact group, the process was saved from failure.

Background and the Negotiation Challenge

The Philippines has experienced internal conflict for over four decades. The violence was primarily related to poor governance that empowered a few at the expense of the rest of the population. As a result, local rebellions against the elites and rivalries between different elite factions cropped up throughout the country. The most powerful and long lasting of these rebellions were a national-level communist-inspired insurgency against the ruling elites and a separatist regional struggle in the southern Bangsamoro region.

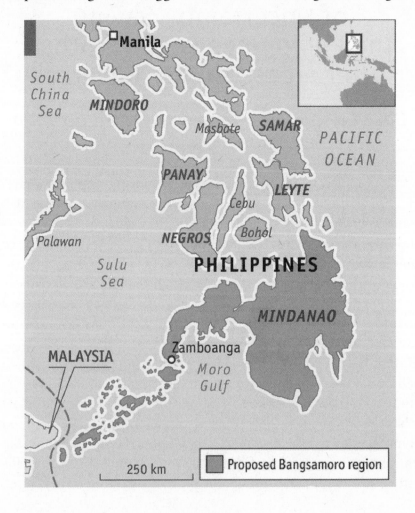

After World War II there was significant discontent emanating from repression of dissent and foreign interference. These two factors led to the first conflict stemming from the creation of the Communist Party of the Philippines (CPP). The CPP tried for many years to overthrow the President Marcos–led government, but did not succeed. After those attempts and the removal of Marcos through popular protests, the CPP changed tactics and engaged in peace talks with the government, which have still not concluded as of this writing.

The second conflict primarily took place in the southern Philippines. The failure of campaigns in the 1960s to recognize local people's rights led to the development of nationalist separatist movements. Since then, various armed groups have fought the government for greater autonomy.

In March 2014 a comprehensive peace agreement was signed between the government and the largest of these groups, the Moro Islamic Liberation Front (MILF),[1] ending a war that killed approximately 150,000 people.[2] While intermittent fighting still occurs with small breakaway groups, the agreement has largely held.

The negotiation in this case focuses on the spring of 2008. In May of that year, representatives from the two parties, the facilitator and members of the international community, civil society, and international media gathered in Kuala Lumpur, Malaysia, to witness what was supposed to be the signing of a historic agreement, the Memorandum of Understanding on Ancestral Domain (MOU-AD), that had just been initialed by the two parties. It was a huge surprise that the parties had reached an agreement.

Only a few years earlier the Philippine government launched a very popular all-out war against the MILF, overrunning their base camp. As a result, the MILF reciprocated asymmetrically with sporadic attacks, including a vicious bombing campaign against Filipino targets and an overseas Embassy. Many in the Philippine Christian community harbored resentment toward the MILF, associating them with international Islamic terrorists, while most Muslim Mindanoans never believed the Philippine government could ever be trusted to sign or implement an agreement following previous failed attempts.

The process leading up to the MOU-AD agreement was shrouded in secrecy because neither party wanted to give the impression it was negotiating with the other side. Very few people knew what was contained in the agreement and most distrusted Malaysian government involvement.[3] When it was publicly announced that the parties had initialed an agreement and planned a formal signing ceremony in Malaysia, many quickly jumped to oppose it, fearing the worst.

To add to the drama, as the Philippine negotiation team was flying with the facilitator from Manila to Kuala Lumpur, the Philippine Supreme Court shockingly issued a temporary restraining order preventing its own government negotiators from the signing of the MOU-AD agreement. The Philippine Office of the President then declared the agreement null and void, leaving those who facilitated and negotiated the agreement in shock and anger (later the Supreme Court would rule that the MOU-AD was unconstitutional). Everyone feared the worst, thinking it would not be too long before massive fighting would return that would probably be worse than before. No one knew when and if the process would ever return.

Preparing to Negotiate

In the dour afternoon of the day of the aborted signing when heads were down and people scrambled even to know if they could return to the Philippines without fear of arrest, the facilitator was asked by the Malaysians and the lead negotiators from the two parties to present a plan B (aka a BATNA). Fortunately a plan B had actually been in the works for some time. Over the previous few years, the group of facilitators, along with the lead negotiators from the two parties, had been working behind the scenes on another possible solution should this agreement fall apart. The reason they engaged in this preventive effort was because there had been a lot of criticism of the existing process for being nontransparent, not inclusive of communities and elected political leaders, and partly facilitated by a third party (aka the Malaysians) not trusted by the Philippine government.[4]

Drawing on previous experience elsewhere, particularly in Aceh, Indonesia, one member of the facilitation team put together ideas on what might be the most appropriate architecture going forward and proceeded to obtain buy-in from the parties. He discreetly vetted these ideas moving it forward, but being very careful not to leak it for fear of upending the existing process or having it get rejected before it had a chance to develop. The parties and the Malaysians all sensed that at some point the process was probably going to need additional international support. It was recognized that, like in other places, any final peace agreement would require some sort of democratic validation, such as a referendum, to give the agreement public legitimacy and therefore national support. A final agreement could not politically, publicly, or legally be signed off behind closed doors by a few representatives from the parties as had often been done in the past.[5]

The Negotiations

After the collapse of the MOU-AD, the facilitator and colleagues had to develop the plan B idea further, make it credible, and get additional buy-in from the rest of the leadership of each party as well as, eventually, public support. The facilitators initiated secret shuttle diplomacy efforts between Manila, Kuala Lumpur, and the MILF base camp in Mindanao, Darapanan. Throughout this period, there was little formal engagement between the parties aside from the Joint Committee for the Cessation of Violence, which maintained some contacts on the ground – mostly sharing information on the security situation.

The ongoing fighting naturally drove hard-liners in both parties to the surface and turned the public even further against the peace process. That made it difficult for either side to publicly support any return to talks. Moreover, arrest warrants had been issued for many commanders in the MILF, making their engagement extremely risky. Politically, it was hard to resume the process as the government began to demand the removal of Malaysia from any talks. With Malaysia in a very difficult position to reengage as part of the facilitation team, much of the work fell to a small nongovernmental organization called the Centre for Humanitarian Dialogue (HD). Legally, the process was also stuck, as the MILF insisted that any new talks recognize the MOU-AD, while the government argued it could not recognize the MOU-AD in the wake of the Supreme Court's ruling that it was unconstitutional. While trying to take the process to a new level, much of the time was also spent trying to prevent the process from regressing as each party began imposing unrealistic conditions that were boxing them into corners.

While it appeared at face value that the peace process was dead, in fact both parties privately recognized that they would eventually need to restart talks. Most likely it would be on the basis of what had been largely agreed before in the MOU-AD. In other words, the end state solution was still largely agreed. Restarting a new process was more about ensuring that this time any agreement would be politically, publicly, and legally viable. Over the course of the next year and a half, the facilitation team went back and forth between Manila, the MILF Camp in

Cotabatu, and Kuala Lumpur trying to find the right formula to make it work this time around.

While the idea of some sort of International Contact Group (ICG) of friendly nations to support the process was gaining traction, the team also needed to address other issues that emerged following the collapse of the MOU-AD. Both sides wanted to avoid that mistake again. The MILF now needed to demonstrate to their constituents that not only would Malaysia remain a key part of the facilitation team, but there would also be a stronger presence of the international community to help guarantee any future agreement would not be rejected as the MOU-AD had been. Moreover, they also needed to reassure their people that they would not abandon the MOU-AD, but would make certain any new process maintained it. It was critical for the MILF to get a deal that was better than their rival, the MNLF, had obtained from the government in 1996 in order to save face.

For the newly elected Philippine government of President Benigno Noynoy Aquino III, they needed to demonstrate a few different dimensions to the agreement, including:

1. A diluted role for Malaysia with friendly international states involved
2. A more inclusive group of elected government officials from Mindanao
3. More openly inclusive of the public's views
4. That the agreement was legally viable and would not end up like the MOU-AD fiasco

During this shuttle diplomacy period, the facilitation team often felt like magicians having to constantly demonstrate new tricks and techniques to get the parties back to the table. It was painful at times and the ongoing fighting and history of failed processes in the Philippines often dampened the facilitator's enthusiasm. However, the team could always see the light at the end of the tunnel.

The process ended up leading to the creation of the ICG as well as commitments by the parties to have a more inclusive and transparent process. They also agreed to a sufficient degree of democratic validation to ensure public buy-in and a process that was more legally and politically viable.

The process was ripe at that time for this type of approach and engagement, but it may not necessarily be appropriate for other processes. The key was the stage the process was in, the willingness of the leaders, and the needs of the people. At that time, the parties needed a small NGO that all the parties, including the facilitator, knew and trusted to discreetly shuttle around and help restart a new process. The ICG did end up playing a very critical role in helping Malaysia and the parties cross the finish line. As Woody Allen once said, "90% of life is showing up." The facilitator and other players showed up at the right time, the right place, and with the right methodology.

Lessons Learned

This case exhibits that a negotiation is never complete until the parties sign on the dotted line. In this example, a deal had essentially been agreed to only to experience a last-minute reversal by one of the parties. Only through foresight and thoughtful planning was a crisis averted. Here are some of the key lessons to grasp.

Lesson 1: Reframing the Problem Helped to Shift from Positions to Interests

Perhaps the most difficult issue was overcoming the MILF's insistence that the MOU-AD be recognized as an agreement between the parties and the government's insistence that it could not be included because the Supreme Court had deemed it unconstitutional. It was difficult for both parties to back down legally, publicly, and politically. The situation had become positional. After much back and forth, it turned out the most obvious solution was actually the most agreeable. By getting beneath these positions to the parties' interests, both entities eventually realized that a joint statement to simply acknowledge the MOU-AD as an initialed and yet unsigned document would be sufficient for them. Once this was achieved, the process could move forward.

Lesson 2: Adaptability and Persistence in the Face of Numerous Obstacles

With the last-minute change by the Philippine Supreme Court, the facilitator and colleagues could very easily have thrown up their hands and given up. After all, this type of change not only poses challenges in the short term, but also the longer term. Signals are sent about intentions when something like this occurs. Instead of taking that tact the team quickly regrouped, adjusted their approach, and fell back on previous work in anticipation of potential problems.

Coupled with this adaptability was persistence. There were times when the process stalled or was rolling back, the fighting wasn't ending, and each side was becoming more and more intransigent. However, the persistence of the facilitators during these difficult times built political capital with the parties. The parties saw that the facilitators were deeply committed, willing to take personal risks, and believed in what they were doing, and this inspired them to stay at the table.

Lesson 3: Building Credibility

To give any new process credibility, the parties requested publicly renowned international leaders to help convince their constituents and colleagues to restart the dialogue. High-profile international engagement is not always welcome, of course. However, as both parties had lost a lot of credibility internally, bringing in external leaders to lay out why the parties should return to the table and how they might do so opened up space for the parties to echo these messages to their constituents.

High-level international experts such as Gerry Kelly, who was a former prisoner, hunger striker, fighter, and negotiator in Northern Ireland for Sinn Fein, as well as his opposite number, Jonathan Powell, the former chief of staff to British Prime Minister Tony Blair who had led the talks on Northern Ireland from the Prime Minister's office, were brought in to share their experiences. These two men were able to talk from the same position that the parties were sitting in and helped them walk through critical moments.[6] Moreover, Teresa Whitfield, who at the time had just published a book entitled *Friends Indeed*, on international third-party engagement and its successes and failures, was asked to share her thoughts with the parties as well. These contributions were critical to bolster the legitimacy and credibility of the idea.

Lesson 4: The Importance of Ownership and the Single-Text Procedure

Finally, the facilitator and team produced an initial draft because it needed to be put on paper. No party to the conflict thought they should be the one to make the first proposal for fear the other side might reject it. This initial proposal was done very carefully and in an impartial manner without any organization's letterhead. After several amendments, the parties worked from one draft – often called a single-text procedure – and ultimately came to agreement on the terms of reference for the ICG.[7] While the facilitation team put forward ideas on names of states, soliciting the states interests, the parties ultimately selected which states and NGOs would be involved. The initial work around on the proposal, combined ultimately with ownership in the process by the parties, proved to be the critical formula for its success.

Notes

1. The Moro National Liberation Front (MNLF) was the mother organization of the breakaway Moro Islamic Liberation (MILF). The MILF split after the 1976 Tripoli peace accords between the MNLF and the Philippine government.
2. This background information came from https://www.peaceinsight.org/conflicts/philippines/
3. The Malaysian government was long accused by the Philippine government of having played a role in earlier supporting Mindanano-based insurgent groups due to the outstanding claims the Philippine government had over Malaysian-controlled Sabah.
4. The stage was actually set for the creation of what would become the International Contact Group as early as 2003 when the Philippine government sent military peacekeepers to monitor the implementation of the Centre for Humanitarian Dialogue led peace process in Aceh, Indonesia. David Gorman oversaw this operation on the ground and established a strong rapport with the then–Philippine ambassador posted to Indonesia during that time, Ambassador Rafael Seguis. Ambassador Seguis recognized the value of the Aceh process architecture and its broad concert of international actors involved in mediating, advising, and implementing the peace process in a way that the Indonesian government could tolerate. The Aceh mediation operation was composed of three layers of international engagement including HD as facilitator, international peacekeepers from the Philippines, Norway, and Thailand, a group of four international states and multilateral institutions (the governments of Japan, the United States, the European Union and the World Bank) that shepherded the process, and a group of three so-called Wise Men who provided advice to the parties. All of these bits of architecture played complementary roles in helping to facilitate and implement the 2002 agreement. The experience had a positive effect on the Philippine ambassador, who would later invite HD to come to the Philippines to help with their peace processes in Mindanao. When he later became Philippine negotiator in the Mindanao peace talks, he needed no convincing to support the creation of the International Contact Group and was instrumental in convincing his government to agree to a new broader and more international architecture.

5. At the invitation of the Philippine government and the Moro National Liberation Front (MNLF) in 2005, one of the facilitators and his organization, the Centre for Humanitarian Dialogue (HD), began its engagement in Mindanao, southern Philippines. The MNLF, led by its chairman, Nur Misuari, had already concluded an autonomy agreement in 1996 with the Philippine government. The 1996 agreement established the Autonomous Region of Muslim Mindanao (ARMM). However, this agreement slowly collapsed, and by 2001 fighting had resumed. As a result, HD was asked by the MNLF and the Philippine government to help restart negotiations around the implementation of the 1996 agreement with the government and to work with the Organization of Islamic Conference, which had facilitated the process before. However, in parallel the increasingly powerful MILF and Philippine government were also engaged in a separate peace process that proposed to go further than the 1996 agreement. It was clear that due to the strength and legitimacy of the MILF on the ground, particularly in mainland Mindanao, that any new agreement would need both the MILF and MNLF to be engaged. As a result, while HD was facilitating meetings between the MNLF and the Philippine government, it also began to liaise with the MILF leadership and the Malaysian facilitator of the MILF peace process, Datu Othman Razak.

   During this period, Othman Razak and the mediator began meeting regularly, updating each other, and sharing information and ideas. As the MILF process struggled at times, they started discussing how to strengthen the process. It was in 2007 that the facilitator from HD was first asked to submit the idea in writing of some sort of International Contact Group. After a green light from the facilitator, the two started discreetly shuttling between a series of Philippine government negotiators and the MILF negotiation team. By the time of the collapse of the MOU-AD on August 5, 2008, there was broad consensus already by the chief negotiators and the facilitator on a way forward.

6. Others included former vice president of Indonesia Yusuf Kalla, former UN mediators Alvaro de Soto and Francesc Vendrell, Free Aceh Movement negotiator and later governor of Aceh, Irwandi Yusuf, and former Palestinian negotiator Omar Dajani.

7. The single-negotiation text procedure was made famous by former US president Jimmy Carter at Camp David when he mediated between the Israelis and Egyptians. The idea is that a single text draft is created and the parties add, subtract, and edit the language until they all can agree to it. This eliminates problems, such as competing proposals and sequencing challenges.

22

Listening Them Down
from a Tree

Based on an interview with Gary McDougall

A crisis negotiator for a police department has many things to consider when a situation arises. Often they do not have a lot of information or time to prepare, so they must rely on training and years of experience to determine what is really going on in a given situation. As in many negotiations, what initially manifests itself as the problem to be discussed is not what truly underlies the negotiation.

When you add in the dynamics of time pressure and the risky potential nature of the outcome, these negotiations challenge a negotiator's skillset to the maximum degree. The case that follows meets all of these criteria and then some.

Background and the Negotiation Challenge

The place was Calgary, Alberta, Canada. The situation occurred a number of years ago. Gary McDougall was at home when he got a call that he frequently gets. "Gary," the dispatcher said, "we

219

have got a situation on the outskirts of downtown Calgary. We need you down there right away." "Okay," Gary replied. "Fill me in as I get my things and get in the car."[1]

As Gary hopped into his car the dispatcher explained the situation. A husband and wife of indigenous origin (Native Canadians), who were in their mid-thirties and were also methamphetamine addicts, were having a life-threatening challenge. The wife, Mary, decided she had had enough of their drug-induced lifestyle and was going to check herself into a rehabilitation clinic to finally get clean. She begged her husband, Arthur, to come with her. She loved Arthur very much, but she just could not continue this way. They needed to shake their drug habit, or she feared that they might not live much longer. Arthur refused repeatedly, despite her many entreaties.

Mary, however, was resolute in how important this was and left on her own and checked herself into the Better Days Rehabilitation Clinic on the edge of downtown Calgary. Arthur, now alone, fumed as he took more methamphetamine. "How could she do this to me?" he thought to himself. "We had this beautiful relationship going and now she had to go and wreck it." His mind began to wander – partly due to the drugs and partly to his overwhelming feelings of anger and frustration toward Mary. He had to teach her a lesson that she would never forget.

Arthur began to craft a plan. He went to his garage and found a length of nylon rope. He tied a noose in it and placed it over his head. It fit – even though it was a bit tight – but it would do the trick. Arthur knew exactly where Mary was because she had called him three times from the clinic begging him to join her. Arthur grabbed the rope and threw it into the backseat of his car. The effects of the methamphetamine had yet to fully wear off, but he was cognizant enough of what he was doing. As he drove slowly to the rehabilitation facility, his mind raced with many different thoughts. When he got close to the facility, he shut off his lights. It was nearly midnight. He had a pretty good sense of where Mary was because she described a beautiful tree that she could see from her window. After parking the car nearby, he sat there smoking what he imagined would be his last cigarette.

As he got out of his old Chevrolet the door creaked loudly. He slammed it shut behind him and then grabbed the rope from the backseat through the open window. A nearby streetlight provided just enough light for him to figure out how to get up the tree Mary had described. He climbed up the tree and put the noose around his neck and tied the other end of the rope to the trunk of the tree.

As all this was happening a young man passed by and stopped. He said, "What are ya doin'?" Arthur gruffly dismissed him, "Go away. This is none of your damn business!" The man, of course, had a pretty good idea what was happening. As he began to walk away, he pulled out his phone and dialed 911. He told the dispatcher what he had seen. They scrambled to get first responders to the scene who engaged in conversations with Arthur to keep him occupied until Gary could arrive. Arthur was clear with them—he was not going to come down out of the tree alive.

Preparing to Negotiate

As Gary drove speedily through the city listening to the dispatcher, many thoughts ran through his mind, as they often did when these kinds of crises arose. Did this man really want to kill himself? If not, why was he *really* doing this? What was driving his behavior? What clues did he get from the story with the dispatcher about Arthur's real underlying interests and intentions?

Gary knew that in these situations time was usually not on his side. When people get into this state of mind, quick action is needed. What is also needed is a lot of listening. The subject in this situation will likely tell him what he needs to know if he can find a way to connect with him. It wouldn't be easy, but this formula had generally worked for him in the past.

When Gary pulled past the rehabilitation clinic, he saw the tree and the silhouette of a man standing on a branch 30 feet above the ground. While he could not see the noose around his neck, he could see the other end of the rope dangling down from the tree and tied around the trunk. As Gary parked his car, he took a deep breath and opened the door, quickly making his way to the base of the tree.

The Negotiation

Gary began the negotiation by identifying himself as being with the police and then engaging Arthur. The two of them had a very lengthy back and forth about what had transpired between Mary and himself early in the day. Arthur spent much of the time talking about how Mary had ruined his life by going to the rehabilitation facility. He kept reiterating that they had such a good life together. Eventually, he shared that all he wanted to do was "this ultimate act that would rock her world."[2] It was Arthur's intent to be hanging in the tree the following morning when Mary arose and opened her curtains. That would send a powerful message to her of how she had ruined his life.

It was also very clear to Gary that Arthur was in a positional negotiation mindset. As he said to Gary, "There is no way you are going to get me out of this tree. The only way I will come down is in a body bag."[3] As the negotiation progressed into the early morning hours, Gary was concerned about Mary waking up and being able to see what was happening outside her window. Gary realized that his only hope was to find a way to shift the conversation to a more interest-based approach. But how?

The weather was cold; it was late October and in that part of the world winter was beginning to blow in. Both Gary and

Arthur were getting cold, which was impacting their desire to find a solution. Gary felt in his heart of hearts that Arthur really wanted to come down and not kill himself. The problem, as Gary surmised, was that Arthur could not come down because he would lose face, and with it, his self-respect. Arthur alluded to that time and again in different but subtle ways.

Gary then reminded himself about the critical importance of inquiry. So he asked this question: "Friend, what would it take for you to come out of that tree?" At first Arthur was silent, but he then spoke assertively. "I will come out of this tree if you can guess my indigenous name." Gary thought to himself, "Hmm. . . that is a tough one, but I wonder what underlies that request." Gary then said, "That seems really important to you." Arthur quickly reiterated, "If you will guess my name I will come out of this tree." Taking a step back, Gary said, "If you give me a few minutes to collect my thoughts, I will do that."[4] Arthur nodded in agreement.

Gary moved away from the scene and called the dispatcher. He asked the dispatcher to call the Rehabilitation Center, wake up Mary, and ask her Arthur's indigenous name. Gary also told the dispatcher to make sure Mary did not go to the window to see what was going on. The dispatcher quickly got to work.

After about three or four minutes the dispatcher spoke to Gary through his earpiece. "His name is Running Buffalo." Gary turned back to Arthur and said, "I think that your name is Running Buffalo."[5] Arthur was silent for a moment and then burst into tears, took the rope off of his neck, and hurried down the tree as fast as he possibly could. When he got down to the ground he fell into Gary's arms and started to cry.

Gary took him to the ambulance to warm him up. When they were sitting in the ambulance Gary looked at Arthur and said, "I have to ask you something. What was behind your desire to have me determine your name? What was that really about?" Arthur looked at him and stated, "Well, I really, really wanted to come down out of the tree, but I felt if I did you would win and I would lose. I needed to find a way to come down on equal footing. I wanted to put you through a hoop so that I could claim a victory and be on par with you."[6] As Gary had pondered, coming down out of that tree equated to a sense of loss for Arthur unless there was something that could be added to the equation.

Lessons Learned

Some fascinating lessons from this case are highlighted explicitly below. While these lessons may seem as if they might only apply to other extreme cases, they have a lot of applicability to many different types of negotiations.

Lesson 1: Listening, Building Rapport, and Getting to Underlying Interests

Information is the currency of negotiation. The way that you solve some of the most intractable problems in negotiation is through asking good questions, listening intently, and building rapport. Such was the case here as Gary went into the situation with a mindset to ask questions to try to get at the suspect's underlying interests. "What is it going to take to get you out of this tree?" Once that question was asked, the door was opened ever so slightly for Arthur to walk through. After Arthur's test to Gary he was able to share his true interests – feeling betrayed and abandoned by his wife. As he said to Gary, "We had this great thing going and Mary took it all away from me."

The idea, as Gary elucidated, is always to get the suspect to talk to you, find places where you can agree in order to build a connection, and then you have to be listening for what is really going on. What is motivating their behavior? Are there recurring themes? Then following that up with active and emphatic listening. As Gary said to Arthur, "It sounds like your wife checking into rehab today was not on your schedule when you woke up." Arthur replied, "Exactly!"[6] In virtually all of the situations Gary finds himself, he clearly sees that people want to be heard, listened to, and then validated. Once those things transpire, good things flow and solutions are more likely to be found.

Lesson 2: Saving Face and Psychological Traps

When Gary arrived on the scene, he had an inkling that Arthur did not really want to kill himself. The more he talked to him the more he realized that Arthur had started down this path, partly while under the influence of drugs, and did not know how to get out of it and how to still save face. Indeed, saving face was the key to this entire ordeal.

When people start down a certain path in negotiation, they often tie themselves to that course of action – sometimes beyond what makes logical sense. Psychological dynamics, such as entrapment, take over. Entrapment is when a person commits to a certain course of action and then gets trapped by the sunk costs and investments they have made.[7] Those sunk costs and investments are not necessarily monetary, but more along the lines of time, commitment, and your reputation. As such, they have a hard time changing course even when it makes sense to do so. In this case Arthur was entrapped and needed a way to save face. What was that way out? He needed a way to win, as he defined it, so he could get on par with Gary as the other negotiator. The question Arthur asked Gary to answer – what his indigenous name was – served that purpose. As Gary deciphered, "This challenge created a task to even the scorecard. Arthur could say, I made that guy do this for me, so now I can come down with dignity."[8]

Lesson 3: The Framing of a Situation and the Application of the Liking Principle

Gary is very careful with his framing in these situations. For example, he never uses the terminology of surrender because it equates to a loss of face. He prefers to use the phrases, "When you come out or when we have an opportunity to see each other." This framing is much more neutral and lacks baggage.

In many ways, framing is key because Gary knows he needs to create a connection with the hostage taker or individual in crisis. While this may seem odd, most people committing these acts will not come out unless they have a level of trust in the other negotiator. For Gary, the theory of liking, as put forth by Cialdini, is key to influencing the other to change course.[9] When liking is achieved, the negotiator has rehumanized a situation desperately suffering from dehumanization.

Lesson 4: Stay Away from Advocacy and Focus More on Inquiry

Finally, hostage takers or people in crisis do not respond to advocacy or telling them why they are wrong. They have been told what to do their whole life and have very likely rebelled against it. Put differently, preaching to them about what they are doing and how wrong it is simply does not work.

In contrast, Gary focuses his efforts on inquiry and trying to determine what is going on and understanding what underlying issue is motivating their behavior. By getting the suspect to share, and get off their chest what it is that is really bothering them, they shift into a place where they can consider a different, more productive, path.

Notes

1. Interview with Gary McDougall.
2. Interview with Gary McDougall.
3. Interview with Gary McDougall.
4. Interview with Gary McDougall.
5. Interview with Gary McDougall.
6. Interview with Gary McDougall.
7. For more on the concept of psychological entrapment, see https://www.beyondintractability.org/essay/sacrifice-trap
8. Interview with Gary McDougall.
9. Cialdini, R. *Influence: The Psychology of Persuasion*, rev ed. (Pearson Books, 2008).

23

Onions and Hostage Negotiations: The Many Layers

Based on an interview with Andy Young

Hostage negotiations are a unique classification of negotiations with many challenges not found in other realms. These processes are typically tense, with high drama, emotions, time pressure, and severe consequences if a solution is not found. This type of negotiation is also complicated by having a number of different parties involved with varied interests and objectives.

While all parties want to see the situation resolved, they often have very different avenues to achieve those objectives. This creates an added dimension for the negotiators involved from a coordination perspective. The case that follows shows the many layers of this type of negotiation and how a process can be managed and coordinated effectively with the best possible outcome secured.

Background and the Negotiation Challenge

In March of 2015 a hostage negotiation situation arose to which the Lubbock County Sheriff's Office (Texas) was dispatched.

The barricaded individual had a number of weapons and the responding deputy learned that the male living at the address had choked a female to the point of dizziness and pointed a shotgun at numerous people nearby. A lone officer, from a neighboring municipality, responded to assist and had a gun pointed at him. He decided to hold his position until other deputies responded. Once the deputies arrived and assessed the scene, the Lubbock County Sheriff's Office SWAT team was activated, and responded. The SWAT response comprised twelve operators, a mental health professional (MHP), and five negotiation personnel. The Texas Department of Public Safety also responded with their regional helicopter overhead for use by the sheriff's office personnel.

The hostage taker in question, Bill, was shuttered up in a house at the end of a 300-foot driveway. This house had some small buildings nearby surrounded by a few trees, but for the most part was in the middle of an open field. There were some neighborhoods about 300 feet away in different directions and deputies soon began evacuating these residences. SWAT team operators and their armored vehicle (called a BATT for short) set up at the end of the driveway with the house off in the distance.

Simultaneously the negotiators began calling the residence and quickly established communication with Bill. Bill was adamant that the police not set foot on his property and was very agitated and emotional. Bill gave off a strong anti-government sentiment and was very angry that things had escalated to the point where the SWAT team was called to the edge of his property. The lead negotiator, Nicole, and her partner, Andy, did an excellent job of allowing Bill to express his anger and sentiments, while also explaining why the police were at the outskirts of his property. One of their goals was to help Bill move from an emotional state to a calmer and more cognitive state. While this was occurring, the state police helicopter circled the property over-head, the loud noise adding tension to the situation.

Bill then got in his car and attempted to leave his property. As he drove down his driveway toward the SWAT team, the state police helicopter, on its own initiative, dropped down in front of him and used its rotor wash in an attempt to dissuade Bill from leaving. Bill decided to turn his car around, went back into his house, and got back on the phone with the negotiators.

When it comes to this type of situation in general, and the subsequent negotiation that transpired, there were numerous direct and indirect parties involved. If all of these parties were not managed effectively, the negotiation was certain to fail. Before delving further, let me provide a brief overview of the direct and indirect parties involved.

Direct parties

1. Nicole was the first direct party, as the lead negotiator for the police. Nicole worked closely and in tandem with Andy, who was the psychological consultant on the team and would advise her on negotiation strategies and on the mental state of the barricaded individual. Nicole met Bill once prior when she responded to a disturbance call at his residence. Nicole stayed on scene during this call for an extra 30 minutes, just so Bill could vent and be heard.

2. Bill was the barricaded individual and hostage taker. It was clear from the situation that Bill had an axe to grind against authority figures. He had some potentially violent tendencies and his own agenda (e.g. to make authority look weak, for authorities to stay off of his property and out of his home, and to have everyone involved play by his rules). Bill was argumentative, let his emotions overwhelm him and guide his behavior, and would at times try to bait responding officers into a fight.

Indirect parties

1. Neighbors of Bill were not directly involved in the situation, but they had been threatened by him and were potential targets of his rage and frustration. There was also an elementary school about a mile away.

2. The Lubbock County Sheriff's Office SWAT team (lead by the SWAT commander) was a key player in this situation. The SWAT team's presence clearly had an impact on what transpired in this case. The SWAT commander and negotiating team consulted each other throughout this incident, kept each other abreast of what was happening, and the SWAT team stood at the ready should they need to help contain the situation.

3. The Texas Department of Public Safety also played an important containment role with the use of their helicopter. At a key point they intervened to keep Bill on his premises, thereby preventing a more chaotic situation from emerging.

The key negotiation task was how to get Bill to give himself up without hurting anyone further, including responding officers. It was not an easy assignment and required patience, humility, rapport building, and an in-depth understanding of Bill and his worldview.

Preparing to Negotiate

As Nicole was on the phone with Bill, Andy considered the situation in front of them and began to assess the dynamics involved. He was particularly focused on the helicopter with all the noise it was creating. Clearly the helicopter was making Bill more and more tense. Negotiators such as Nicole and Andy are always looking for a way to influence and change a situation that appears as though it could escalate. Andy asked the SWAT commander about setting the negotiation up so that Nicole could offer to move the helicopter away. Knowing that Bill seemed to espouse strong anti-government sentiments, withdrawing the state police helicopter could help Bill feel more at ease and might even suggest that he had some power in the situation. Furthermore, this offer could easily help build rapport, credibility, and trust between Bill and Nicole. Andy asked to share this idea, and reasoning, with the SWAT commander. Incidentally the SWAT commander had previously attended a 40-hour negotiation course, an element of which was how to discuss decision making with other team members in a straightforward, open, and collaborative manner.

The SWAT commander, who was standing in a circle of other commanders, was approached by Andy. The SWAT commander was busy with radio communications and consulting with his superiors, along with supervising the SWAT team and making plans for how to tactically handle this situation. The commander had been updated on the progress of the negotiations and had been briefed on Bill's desire not to have people come on his land, along with his general attitude toward authority figures. The commander was in the challenging position of having to balance this perspective against the likelihood of Bill getting in his car and trying to flee the scene again, thereby endangering his neighbors and even the elementary school down the street.

The commander began considering moving the SWAT team onto Bill's property and getting them between Bill and his car. Both Nicole and Andy knew this move would infuriate Bill and would likely cause the negotiations to break down – perhaps even inciting Bill to violence. Nicole and Andy saw the critical nature of deescalating the situation as soon as possible, but they also had to balance this with keeping the public safe and containing Bill.

The commander listened to the plan and then asked Andy what he thought about moving the tactical team onto Bill's land and getting between Bill and his car. "Should we risk him trying to drive off again? Should we honor his request not to 'trespass' onto his land and thereby keep negotiations going well? How bad will this action negatively affect our negotiations?"[1] The group discussed it all and came up with a plan that tried to honor every element. What if Nicole offered to move the helicopter and then did so? After that Nicole could let Bill know that the SWAT team was going to have to move onto his property, and she could help Bill work through his anger and questions about this. She could attempt to explain why this was necessary, and doing so would help Bill continue to see Nicole as honest, helpful, and even trustworthy. The SWAT commander was also concerned with the safety of his officers as they moved onto Bill's property and typically would not want Bill to know what was about to happen. However, in this case, due in part to the open field, and in part to the situation with Bill, the SWAT commander opted to concede this point with the overall picture and goals in mind.

The Negotiation

Nicole very effectively framed the offer to move the helicopter for Bill. After Bill said he would like this very much, the helicopter rose to about 1,000 feet via the SWAT commander's orders. It became much quieter on the scene and the tension noticeably subsided. Nicole then explained what the SWAT team was about to do and why they had to do this. Bill was indeed angry and vented to Nicole. She did not try to stop his venting, but rather allowed Bill to get out all his frustrations and let Bill know she understood where he was coming from.[2] Nicole validated his feelings while also not taking his side or taking his venting personally.

Nicole had come to understand one of Bill's goals, which was to make the authorities look weak or to bait them into a fight by provoking them. Nicole was very effective at getting Bill to talk to her and focus solely on her – blocking out all else that was transpiring. This tactic would only last for short periods, especially because the men on the SWAT team were also "negotiating" with him, both verbally and through their actions. The SWAT negotiating team leader talked with the tactical commander about this problem, and the commander was assured by his people that they were not talking with Bill. This was not confirmed by the negotiators, however, because they could clearly hear someone from the SWAT team talking with Bill. While coordination was mostly effective, there were certainly some small missteps along the way that needed to be managed. Finally, Bill came back and focused on talking with Nicole as he had before, once the SWAT commander issued an order not to talk with Bill unless he was coming out. As part of their conversation, Bill used the term "giving himself up" for the first time. This was a breakthrough and came as a result of the progression of the overall situation, but also the trust and rapport Nicole developed with Bill.

As the negotiation continued, Bill stated to Nicole that he would give himself up to her, but not to "any of those SWAT guys." It seems that Bill's goal was to make himself seem in charge of his capitulation so he could save face. Nicole was satisfied with this plan, but again had to coordinate with the command and tactical members, especially because this plan was not a "normal way" of doing things in such a dangerous situation. Typically, the SWAT team takes an armed subject into custody, so once again the team had to navigate uncharted waters and be flexible. Everyone was concerned about Nicole's safety and wanted to balance this with resolving this situation peacefully.

As the situation progressed, the negotiated plan was that the BATT would come to the end of Bill's driveway, pick up Nicole, and take her up the driveway to Bill's house. Nicole would proceed to get out of the BATT and stand next to the driver's side with another SWAT officer next to her. At that point Bill would come to her and be taken into custody. The commander was willing to do this in part because there were a number of SWAT operators in position to protect Nicole. Bill assured Nicole that he would not have any weapons on him.

Nicole, Andy, a driver, and the SWAT negotiating team leader loaded up and headed to the end of the driveway. As Andy recalled, "We waited. And waited. And had a little trouble with our radios. Eventually we learned that the SWAT team did not want to lose their tactical advantage by moving the BATT down the road to pick up Nicole. So instead, we were to drive down the driveway and park behind the BATT."[3] Nicole was on the phone with Bill as they learned of this change and he objected to it. Bill abruptly said he needed to talk to one of his friends and hung up as the vehicle they were in was moving down the driveway. Prior intelligence had been relayed to them, by the outer perimeter, that Bill had friends of his own on the scene.

Nicole called Bill back and was successful in getting him on the phone about the time they were all getting out of the vehicle. Andy climbed into the passenger side seat of the BATT and had a megaphone available to him in case it was needed. Bill walked toward Nicole, but the SWAT rescue team moved up in an effort to cut off Bill from being able to regain access into his residence. In that moment, everyone thought everything that had been worked for over the last few hours was going to be lost. When Bill saw the SWAT team moving in, he started yelling at the rescue team, while also heading back toward his front door. It was obvious to everyone that Bill would beat the SWAT team to the door, so the SWAT team froze. For some reason Bill also froze. At the same time Nicole kept talking, and once again, worked to keep Bill's attention on her. Eventually Bill shifted his attention from the SWAT team to Nicole. As he did, he walked toward her and allowed her to put handcuffs on him. A collective exhale was taken by everyone involved.

After Bill was taken into custody, the SWAT team entered Bill's house to clear it and make sure it was safe. The negotiating team watched the SWAT team enter the house and then quickly evacuate. Earlier in the standoff Bill had turned the gas burners on his stove on, and lit candles throughout his living room. The assumption was that, when Bill realized Nicole was coming up to the house to take him into custody, he went through the house and blew out the candles and turned off the gas. When the SWAT team entered his house, the smell of gas was still apparent. It seems Bill's earlier promises to Nicole not to hurt her were true, as were his threatening statements toward the SWAT team. It also seems clear in hindsight that this situation could easily have gone very wrong, especially if egos and arguments had been part of this process and if Nicole had not been very adept at connecting with Bill.

As an interesting and final side note. Bill made bail the next day and went to breakfast. There, at a local restaurant, were two sheriff's deputies who had nothing to do with the events of the previous day. Bill bought their breakfast as he left for home. This may have been Bill's final, symbolic demonstration of dominance over the Lubbock County Sheriff's Office – or something else entirely.

Lessons Learned

There are a number of lessons to draw from this precarious and tense negotiation that fortunately ended well for all involved.

Lesson 1: Managing Many Players and Keeping Them Coordinated

First was the ability to manage a team with very different interests and mindsets. Nicole and the negotiation commander were viewing everything through a negotiation lens. Andy, while understanding the negotiation aspect, viewed the situation through a psychological lens. The Department of Public Safety and the SWAT team's lens was safety and security. The challenge of coordinating all of these different lenses and negotiating in this context was very difficult, but was handled as effectively as it could have been.

Lesson 2: Understanding the Psychological Dimensions Involved

Second was the empathy that Nicole and Andy practiced, while also staying focused on the underlying psychological interests that were driving Bill's behavior. Nicole and Andy understood early on that Bill had a negative view of government and public officials, but also that he had a strong desire to be heard, not look weak, and to save face as part of any deal to come out. As Andy noted afterwards, "Had anyone's egos gotten involved, be it the sheriff, the SWAT commander, other brass on scene, Nicole, me, or our negotiating team leader, we believed this callout would have ended very badly, and possibly in an explosion of Bill's house."[3]

Lesson 3: Going to the Balcony to Manage Emotions

Third, due to the high stress and emotions involved, Nicole did a very good job of going to the balcony, so that her emotions did not get the better of her. There were ample opportunities for that to happen based on Bill's personality and the frequent rants that he went on. At different points in the case Nicole could also be seen taking Bill to the balcony to calm him down. In the end, she got to a point with Bill where he trusted her, and the only thing that kept the situation from escalating out of control was her ability to keep him focused on the end goals and a peaceful solution for all involved.

Lesson 4: Using the Ethos, Pathos, and Logos of Persuasion

Fourth, Nicole was adept at using ethos, pathos, and logos in her interactions with Bill. As you can read from their interactions,

Nicole particularly understood the value of pathos with Bill. Without the emotional bond that they had formed, as Andy noted, the situation could have ended up much differently. Nicole, with the help of Andy, also did not feel as though she had to respond to Bill's rants, but rather to simply listen through them for what were the underlying issues to be addressed.

Lesson 5: Keeping Ego in Check

Finally, another factor in this scenario was how easily ego could have become a significant problem in this negotiation if people had not been conscious of Bills' underlying issues and motivations. This challenge occurred at many levels during the negotiation. For example, the tactical and command staff could easily have let their ego become a factor in their decision making and not want to give Bill what he needed in order to give himself up. This was particularly difficult because Bill could be quite disrespectful and gifted at getting a negative reaction out of people. Furthermore, the SWAT team could also let ego become a part of their decision making if they thought they should be the ones to negotiate or if they just wanted to teach Bill a lesson. The negotiating team was successful in selling the plan to have Bill taken into custody by Nicole, due in part to the SWAT commander checking his ego at the door and considering all the factors at play.

Notes

1. Interview with Andy Young.
2. It is important to note that she used empathy, or understanding, and not sympathy, which would be agreement. She explained to Bill she knew where he was coming from, not that she agreed with his perspective. That is a line that is important for hostage negotiators not to cross.
3. Interview with Andy Young.

24

What Does Success Look Like for a Hostage Negotiator?

Based on an interview with Harry Drucker

Success in negotiation in general is an interesting question. Some people will say success is reaching agreement. Others will say success is not just an agreement, but an agreement that stands the test of time. Still others will say success is about meeting their objectives as best as possible. And finally, there are those that will look more at their performance and define success as to whether they did the best they could in a given situation.

With all of those views on success, what happens if we drop that concept into a particular context – namely, hostage negotiation. What does success look like in these situations? Furthermore, how does a hostage negotiator know if they have been successful? How can they judge their own performance? To answer these questions there are two places to look. The first is outcome and the second is process.

When one looks at outcomes there is plenty of data to analyze, as hostage negotiation expert Randall Rogan has done. After assessing the long-term data around hostage negotiations, Rogan claims that 85 to 90% of these kinds of situations are resolved nonviolently through a verbal agreement.[1] It is hard to argue with that statistic!

Conversely, when it comes to process, not only do hostage negotiators work with incomplete information like the rest of us, but they also have very little control over the outcome. These negotiators can take the same exact approach and use the same exact actions in two similar cases and arrive at completely differently conclusions. This is due to the hostage taker and their objectives in a particular negotiation as well as to varying dynamics.

Through the case below, let's look at success from these different angles to see what can be gleaned.

Background and the Negotiation Challenge

Danny Kai Chao, 27, walked into a Cathay Bank at Atlantic Boulevard and Alhambra Road in Alhambra, California. It was 9:30 in the morning. He claimed he had a gun in his pocket. He also demanded $50,000.

Chao quickly took nine hostages as part of his efforts to rob the bank. All of the hostages were bank employees. Unbeknownst to Chao, one of the employees tripped a silent alarm that alerted the police. Within a short period of time, there were police resources from throughout the region at the scene. Chao peered out at the scene and began to get very nervous.

Part of the reason Chao was nervous was that he was far from a professional hostage taker. To this point in his life Chao had no criminal record. He had gotten himself in substantial trouble and he owed some shady characters a considerable amount of money. His life was in jeopardy if he did not pay them back quickly and he was at a point of desperation.[2] As he thought about it, he just wanted to pay his debt and then get on with his life.[3]

Negotiating with someone in this state of anxiety posed numerous challenges. Clearly Chao was in the here and now and was not thinking about the longer-term consequences of his actions. It also appeared as if Chao had not really thought through his plan, how he might pull all of this off, and how he would disappear back into society. From a negotiation perspective, those dynamics were both helpful and problematic.

Preparing to Negotiate

When it comes to this type of negotiation, a significant amount of specific preparation is hard to do before the situation begins to unfold. As a result, there is considerable training and work to be done well beforehand, so everyone is clear what their role is as they arrive on the scene. This is critical because negotiation in hostage situations is very much a team effort. Furthermore, hostage negotiators are trained in a behavioral change method and have to put that into practice from the very start of their interaction with the hostage taker. Both of these preparatory actions require more detailed analysis, along with a few other important anecdotes that take place during this phase.

As was alluded to above, because hostage negotiations happen with a team, it is essential that everyone know their roles and responsibilities. To begin with, there is the primary negotiator, whose job is to communicate important ideas about what they will and will not do and to build a relationship with the hostage taker.[4] In addition to the primary negotiator, there is a negotiating partner, someone who can swap in should the primary negotiator get fatigued or if the situation is not progressing well. This negotiating partner also serves as someone who the primary negotiator can bounce ideas off of as part of the process. There is also a person tasked with gathering intelligence about the situation so they can brief the team as they come on scene. Finally, the last key role is the team leader – or the decision maker. The team leader is not directly involved in the negotiation per se, but is listening in, taking a more dispassionate approach, and making the big picture decisions based on what they are hearing. This negotiation team has to be coordinated with other aspects of the overall situation, such as with the local law enforcement and SWAT teams.

Due to the lack of preparation time hostage negotiators have to fall back on their training and experience. A significant part of their training is encapsulated in the Federal Bureau of Investigation's Behavioral Change Stairway Model (BCSM). This model lays out the process that negotiators are to adhere to in their high-stakes negotiations. The model is as follows:

Step 1: Active Listening. This first step involves a number of techniques aimed at establishing a relationship between the hostage negotiator and the hostage taker. These techniques include open-ended questions, paraphrasing their understanding of the hostage taker's story, identifying the hostage taker's emotions, and knowing when to pause the conversation to give time for the parties to think and reflect.

Step 2: Empathy. The second step is all about empathizing with the other side as a way of building the relationship. Empathy signals to the hostage taker that their perceptions and feelings are understood. Tone of voice is key here because it conveys an interest and concern in them.

Step 3: Rapport. The third step is all about increasing trust between the parties. The negotiator focuses on ways to help the other save face, continually reframing the situation, and exploring areas of common ground.

Step 4: Influence. After step 3 is done, a hostage negotiator is able to make suggestions to the other side and explore potential solutions. They need to think here about what will be persuasive to the hostage taker and why. Much of this comes from inquiry and drawing out information.[5]

Step 5: Behavioral Change. The last step in the model is for the hostage negotiator to propose solutions that will garner the desired behavioral change.[6]

This behavioral change model is sequential. If a negotiator skips a step, the hostage taker often sees through the model and feels as if they are being presented something that is disingenuous.

Drucker shares two other important points that are worth noting during this phase of the process. Clearly a negotiator needs to know what the crime in question is, but it is almost better not to know too much because the goal is to build rapport with the hostage taker. It is also often wise not to discuss the crime the hostage taker is committing because it may remind them of the potential consequences of what they are doing. Thus, it is preferable to deal with the immediate issue and needs of the hostage taker in the moment.

Connected to the previous point is the importance of not telling a hostage taker what they should do. Police in general are trained to be problem solvers, but solving the hostage taker's problem through direction is the last thing a hostage taker wants from the person on the other end of the phone. If a person has been a career criminal all they have been hearing is what they should and should not do from authority figures. Hostage negotiators, instead, are trained to listen and engage in productive inquiry.

The Negotiation

For the first two hours of the hostage situation Chao would not speak directly to the hostage negotiators. He even told them initially that his name was James. The false name and having the hostages speak directly to the hostage negotiators was a way of keeping some distance between himself and them. He also did this because his plan for the day was not going as he envisioned.

Once the hostage negotiators did get Chao on the phone there was a lot of initial bargaining of hostages and what it would take to get them released. Eventually through an act of good faith, Chao released two of the hostages. As the hostages came out, they spoke to the hostage negotiation team and explained to them that Chao was polite, they never felt threatened, and they never saw a gun. This helped the negotiation team get a sense of what they were dealing with, which was not a hardened criminal but likely a person acting out of desperation.

With this new information the hostage negotiation team began to notice that Chao seemed a bit disorganized. They also noticed that there was a back-room window that could make for a convenient exit if Chao got distracted. As the negotiator continued to engage Chao in what he really wanted, six additional hostages escaped through that back-room window. As Sgt. David Nater, a spokesman for the Alhambra Police Department, stated, "He was on the phone, and he looked around and realized there were no hostages. He didn't come well prepared, and he's not very well versed in bank robbery methods of business."[7], While Chao was engaged with the hostage negotiator, the final hostage saw an opportunity and ran out the front door.

Once all the hostages were out, the hostage negotiators could breathe a sigh of relief and turn their attention to what Chao really wanted and what was happening to him in this situation.[8] The hostage negotiator in this case followed the BCSM process carefully – beginning with some core elements of active listening and then moving right into empathy. Metaphorically speaking, this process disarmed Chao in the manner intended and the conversation shifted to how to get him to come out.

Through their discussions it became very clear that Chao was concerned about saving face. He knew the news media was there and he was the story of the day. As the news helicopters circled overhead, he asked if the police could have them removed so viewers would not see his face. As he alluded to in the conversations, but explained more clearly later, he did not want to bring shame to his family.

Chao was also worried about being physically assaulted by the SWAT team. The hostage negotiator promised him this would not happen if he came out peaceably, and she lived up to her word. Chao trusted her because she built the kind of rapport envisioned in the BCSM. One of the most powerful things she said to him was, "This is not the end of your life. You can survive this."[9] That struck a chord with him.

As Drucker mentioned, the primary negotiator used a tone with Chao that was very effective. In fact, at a few different points in the process she used poorly chosen phrases that normally cause hostage negotiators to cringe when uttered. For example, she stated, "We can end this in another ten minutes," and "You can surrender anytime." Talking about ending things is often not advisable because it could give the idea to the hostage taker of taking their own life. Similarly, hostage negotiators don't use the term "surrender" anymore because it comes across as a loss or defeat – something the hostage taker is desperately trying to avoid. All that stated, due mostly to her tonality these phrases did not throw the process off in the way it might have had the rapport she built not existed.[10]

At approximately 4:45 p.m., Chao walked outside and gave himself up to a sheriff's department SWAT team. Detectives said Chao took $6,000 from tellers and the bank vault, but he left it behind when he walked out of the bank. Chao was booked on suspicion of kidnapping for ransom and robbery.

Lessons Learned

Similar to the other hostage negotiation cases in this book, this example required the coordination of many different moving parts and the need to delve under the surface to understand what was really motivating the hostage taker. When that information was unearthed, the negotiation could progress toward a solution. Here are some of the key reasons why that transpired.

Lesson 1: To Define Success, Think Process as much as Outcome

As Drucker explained, "You can do the exact same thing in two hostage negotiation situations. In one instance the hostage taker comes out and the situation is resolved peaceably. In another the hostage taker ends up killing themselves or commits some other act of violence. You, as the hostage negotiator, did nothing different. So what does success really look like?"[11]

In these types of negotiations so much of the outcome is out of your control. There is little doubt that when humans are in crisis it is very difficult to control what happens in the end. These negotiations take turns that you simply cannot anticipate. The best judge of success, as Drucker explained is, "Did you do everything you could during the process? Did you follow the right steps? If so, that is really all you can do and how success should be measured."[12]

Lesson 2: Negotiation Jujitsu in Practice

In the book *Getting to Yes*, the authors talk about a concept called "Negotiation Jujitsu," which is the art of countering "the basic positional moves of bargaining in ways that direct their attention to the merits."[13] The idea is not to criticize or reject their position, which will only make them defensive. When they attack your position or approach, do not push back. Instead deflect their attack against the problem. As Fisher and Ury elucidated, "As in the Oriental martial arts of judo and jujitsu, avoid pitting your strength against theirs directly; instead, use your skill to step aside and turn their strength to your ends. Rather than resisting their force, channel it into exploring interests, investing options for mutual gain."[14]

Once you have done that the other moves involved in Negotiation Jujitsu are:

1. Don't defend your ideas; invite criticism.
2. Recast an attack on you as an attack on the problem.
3. Ask questions and pause.

When Negotiation Jujitsu is applied to this example it is clear that the hostage negotiators used Negotiation Jujitsu and these tactics. The hostage taker is expecting the hostage negotiator to say things such as "Come out with your hands up." Rather they are met with phrases such as "Sounds like you are having a tough day." As one of Drucker's colleagues, Gary McDougall, puts it, "They are expecting to get Arnold Schwarzenegger on the other end of the phone and they get Mr. Rogers."[15] This immediately takes the hostage taker aback and changes the conversation in a direction where rapport can be built. The hostage negotiator is trying to move from officer and suspect to a new and different relationship.

Lesson 3: Excessive Empathy

One of the problems that hostage negotiators encounter is what might be termed excessive empathy. This is borne out in statements from the hostage negotiator to the hostage taker where the hostage negotiator states, "I know how you feel." The reality is the hostage negotiator does not know how the hostage taker feels because they have never truly been in their shoes. Drucker explained that you have to be careful of not crossing a certain line where you try too hard to empathize and it backfires – doing more harm than good.[16]

Notes

1. Rogan's research can be found at https://www.newswise.com/articles/as-hostage-situation-continues-crisis-expert-says-85-to-90-percent-of-crisis-negotiations-are-resolved-nonviolently

2. In an interview Drucker did with Chao seven years later, Drucker learned that Chao came from a Taiwanese family with their heritage steeped in face saving. With his nefarious dealings he did not want to bring shame on his family and actually contemplated committing suicide so he would not cause them that pain. Furthermore, the hostage negotiator who worked most closely with Chao was at the interview. Drucker asked him if he was disappointed that he never got to meet her as he had asked. Chao replied that there was never a time frame to that meeting and she had now fulfilled her promise.

3. Winton, R., and L. Kay, "Standoff Ends Bank Robbery," https://www.latimes.com/archives/la-xpm-2002-jan-30-me-bank30-story.html

4. In addition to these members of the team, mental health professionals are increasingly being integrated into the process, given the high degree of issues with mental health in this context.

5. This step in the process draws heavily on the theory of liking as espoused by Robert Cialdini in his book *Influence: The Psychology of Persuasion*.

6. "Behavioral Change Stairway Model," https://viaconflict.wordpress.com/2014/10/26/the-behavioral-change-stairway-model/

7. Winton, R., and L. Kay, "Standoff Ends Bank Robbery," https://www.latimes.com/archives/la-xpm-2002-jan-30-me-bank30-story.html

8. In this case little was known about Chao and his motives since he had no previous criminal record.

9. Interview with Harry Drucker.

10. The hostage negotiator built such a strong rapport with him that he wanted to thank her for meeting his concerns when he came out but was unable to do so in all of the commotion. Note 2 explains what ultimately transpired.

11. Interview with Harry Drucker.

12. Drucker shared that more and more work is being done related to mental illness and experts from that realm are being more integrated into the process so they can point out these kinds of dynamics as the process is unfolding.

13. Fisher, R., and W. Ury, *Getting to Yes: Negotiating Agreement Without Giving In* (New York, Penguin Books, 1981), p. 108.

14. Ibid.

15. Interview with Harry Drucker.

16. Interview with Harry Drucker.

25

What's in a Name – and How Do You Negotiate It?

Anonymous contribution

Names are how organizations identify themselves to the world and how they convey quite a bit about the mission of the organization. The interesting thing about names is that they can be shared, to a degree. Sometimes, however, sharing a name causes more challenges than it is worth. So if two organizations share a similar name and have to negotiate, who gets to use that contested name and how do they go about figuring out that dilemma?

In this negotiation, two nonprofit organizations had very similar names that ended up being problematic and necessitated a change. One of the organizations had the trademark and the power. The other did not. The win-lose solution, therefore, appeared to be fairly simple. Yet in the end, with the help of a mediator, the parties reached an unexpected mutually beneficial outcome that required counterintuitive thinking, challenging assumptions, and a simple question.

Background and the Negotiation Challenge

This negotiation scenario was shared by someone who worked at a law firm and who was serving their client in a pro bono capacity. The client, who we will call Life Care International (LC), was involved in humanitarian work and the delivery of aid after natural disasters. LC engaged in work all around the world and deployed in rapid fashion to help those in need. They had been operating globally for many years without a problem.

At a certain point LC ended up in a major city in a Slavic country delivering much-needed aid after a natural disaster. While they were working in this city, they encountered another nonprofit organization called Life Care International for the Benefit of Children (LCIBC). This nonprofit organization was much smaller and did a different type of work – primarily helping children in need of medical care. Both entities were known in their respective spheres as simply Life Care.

As they both worked in this city, confusion began to take hold. At first the problem was trivial. The occasional phone call to the wrong office. A sporadic inquiry from the media was made to the wrong entity. However, it got worse and more frequent over time, with people who were seeking to connect with one nonprofit contacting the other nonprofit seeking their help, donations intended for one entity ended up with the other organization, and so on. What began to emerge was a classic trademark dispute.

In trademark law a dispute arises when there is some confusion between one entity that legally holds the name and another that does not. The issue can be intentional or not, but the key element in a trademark conflict is the confusion aspect.

It turns out that LCIBC had been around longer and held the trademark. Due to the confusion both were experiencing, LCIBC eventually asked LC to change their name. This is where the negotiation ensued, as neither wanted to change their name given the sunk costs and investment they both had in their name and, more importantly, their identity. The legal reality, however, was that LCIBC held the trademark so they did not need to change their name. LC, which was a much bigger entity and worked globally, struggled with the notion of changing their name because they were so much bigger and had developed a global brand. Given all the marketing and branding work that would be needed under a new name, LC would not be able to afford the name change and would likely have to shut down.

Preparing to Negotiate

At first the two parties tried to work things out amicably – neither really wanted to engage in a lawsuit. That seemed to run counter to their nonprofit orientation of making a difference in the world. However, neither party was willing to budge from their positions. LC worked closely with their pro bono lawyers to try to figure out a solution. LCIBC did the same, but to no avail – at least initially.

As the pro bono law firm came onboard, a very strange dynamic took hold. Neither nonprofit wanted to engage in a lawsuit. They both wanted to get back to doing their work and move beyond this. Practicality kept getting in the way, however.

As the parties prepared to negotiate, they sought different ways to solve the problem, but simply could not find a viable answer.

The Negotiation

After quite a bit of positional back and forth the pro bono law firm and the other law firm representing LCIBC were at a loss as to how to solve the issue between the nonprofits. At that point one party suggested a mediator be brought in to help. The other agreed.

During the course of the mediation, the mediator eventually asked LCIBC a slightly counterintuitive question given they held the trademark. "How important is your name to you?" It was a very interesting question that stopped the lawyers for LCIBC in their tracks and seemed to shift the conversation to a different and unexpected place. After giving it some thought, LCIBC responded by saying that their name was actually really long and, even though they held the trademark, they would consider changing it. They explained further that their name really did not effectively describe the core of their work and they would be amenable to something else. The question was, what?

The mediator then suggested the following to LCIBC "What if LC paid you to change your name?" There was silence in the room as the parties considered the out of the box suggestion. After a few moments they both realized that the proposed solution might actually break the deadlock. In turned out that solution would be much cheaper and easier for LCIBC to do than the other way around. Interestingly, and what made this solution that much more effective, was the fact that LC had insurance that would not have been enough to pay for their own name change, but would be enough to pay for LCIBC's. Thus, in the end, a creative solution was found out of what seemed like a no-win situation for LC and an uncomfortable one for LCIBC.

Lessons Learned

This case yields some really intriguing lessons, particularly when negotiating parties are willing to find a solution but are stuck in positional ways of viewing the negotiation process.

Lesson 1: What Lies Beneath Is the Key

First, this example beautifully highlights the distinction between positions and interests. On the one hand, LCIBC's position was very clear – LC needed to change its name because it was simply creating too much confusion between the public and the two organizations. Further, since they held the trademark the impetus for change needed to come from LC. On the other hand, LC's position was also clear. They understood the problem and their obligation to be the ones to change, but doing so would very likely put them out of business. After a fairly exhaustive search for a solution between the parties and their lawyers, a mediator was brought in and clearly grasped the positions, but also probed the underlying interests. Taking a new line of questioning led to the next lesson.

Lesson 2: Reframing the Problem in a Counterintuitive Manner

Second, the mediator brought in some very innovative and creative thinking by flipping the problem on its head. Instead of seeing the problem as something the defendant (LC) had to fix on their own, the mediator reframed the problem as a joint one. This perspective freed the mediator to ask some thought-provoking questions, leading to the creative idea of LCIBC changing their name due to their size and having LC pay for it.

Lesson 3: The Value of an Outside Perspective

Third, picking up from the last point, another key lesson of this case is the role of an outsider. When an outsider can come in and work with the parties, they bring a new and fresh perspective – one that challenges some of the fundamental assumptions being made about what is and is not possible. By pushing against the assumption that the only way the problem would be solved was by actions from the defendant, the mediator focused on the underlying interests and found a solution.

Lesson 4: Just Because You Have the Power and the Right Does Not Mean That Is Always the Best Solution

Finally, this case also exhibits how, when one party has power and rights (in the form of the trademark), exercising those rights might not be their best avenue to success. In this scenario LCIBC eventually took a power- and rights-based approach and could have gotten what they wanted. However, there was an ethical dimension that LCIBC struggled with when it came to putting LC out of business. Thus, it seems LCIBC and LC were much better served through an interest-based approach that enabled them both to keep doing the good work they were engaged in, but also solved the problem causing the confusion.

26

Gold Ink, Presidential Letterhead, and Agenda Framing in Contract Negotiations

Based on an interview with Noam Ebner

Contracts are a very familiar realm to most people when thinking about negotiation. At one point or another in the course of people's careers they must negotiate a contract related to a job or services to be rendered. Too often many people fail to really read the contract carefully or to negotiate the terms. This is the case because those people don't think that it is possible to negotiate or don't realize the underlying dimensions involved that are swaying them in a certain direction.

Many of the clauses in contracts are far from innocuous when you read them carefully and think through the implications. Further, the way a contract is written subtly frames issues in a certain manner. That was the reality in the example below, where the person involved initially did not think to negotiate the terms of the contract in front of him. As time and the relationship progressed, he came to see how the contract was delineated in specific ways and how he could assert for his interests in a way that was reasonable to him and not off-putting for his negotiating partner.

Background and the Negotiation Challenge

About twenty years ago, a colleague we will call Meyer was working as an attorney, a mediator, and an adjunct professor of mediation and negotiation in Israel. Given the somewhat limited market for mediation and mediation teaching in Israel at the time, Meyer was happy to receive an offer to teach as a visiting professor at a university in Turkey, which had just established a graduate degree program in conflict resolution.

Meyer made annual visits to this university for five years, and continued to teach occasional courses there for a decade longer. During this period, he negotiated the terms of his contracts on multiple occasions. Some of the major negotiations he engaged in are detailed below and the evolution of his negotiation approach over time is revealed.

Preparing to Negotiate

In Meyer's initial consideration leading up to discussing terms of employment, he recognized that he had no objective criteria for his value and compensation. As he candidly admitted, "I had no experience with this sort of engagement – a ten-week visit to another country to teach a graduate course – and neither did anyone in my network."[1] Meyer had visited Turkey once, but had no sense of the local salary scale. As a result, when considering salary and terms, he worked off of subjective calculations such as "What do I need to cover my family's expenditures during this period?" and "What opportunities am I giving up locally, being in another country?"[2]

When the dean of the school reached out to Meyer to make an offer approaching the lowest end of the range he had reached through his calculation, he accepted the monetary terms without further negotiation: $10,000 to teach a three-credit course, a round-trip ticket, and on-campus lodgings. In turn, the dean accepted Meyer's request that he teach the course in a concentrated manner over a period of 10 weeks rather than the standard 14 weeks.

As Meyer shared "In this first negotiation, my lack of information worked against me. With no knowledge of objective criteria, I had no informational leverage. With no relationship with the university or the dean beyond a couple of emails, I had no relational safety net to fall back on."[3] So, having no familiarity with professional or academic culture in Turkey, only an assumption that it was not the culture Meyer had encountered in Istanbul's Grand Bazaar, he did not know whether bargaining would be an appropriate approach to take. While the offer barely satisfied his monetary needs – really, *barely* satisfied them – he decided not to push the issue. Instead, he focused on his intangible interests of working internationally, varying his inroads to academia, reducing his time away from home, and having an adventure. As a result, he limited his negotiation to lower-risk topics of scheduling. That fall, Meyer spent 10 delightful weeks in Turkey.

While, overall, this deal certainly resulted in a mutual gain of sorts, during Meyer's stay in Turkey he realized that the sum he had agreed to was less than he actually needed, less than what others made, and, probably, less than what he could have gotten had he negotiated. Meyer determined that should he get invited back, the process would be different and he would do his best to increase the monetary value he received. While the first negotiation above began his adventure, the real negotiation commenced heretofore.

The Negotiation

Several months later, the dean contacted Meyer again, asking if he would return to teach the following autumn. In fact, there was very little asking involved; the offer to return was made by mailing him a signed contract, a replication of the previous years, for his signature, and a brief email asking Meyer to be on the lookout for it and to return it as soon as possible. Meyer did return the contract for the dean's consideration, having made some changes, including crossing out the sum and noting that he would like a raise and an extra round-trip airline ticket.

This set of actions led to a more substantive email negotiation. Meyer asked for more money, explaining that the previous sum did not meet his needs for such a prolonged absence from his activities in Israel, and noting to the dean that he knew of others on an out-of-the-ordinary contract, such as his, who received more in compensation. As Meyer explained, "This was a somewhat fuzzy use of an objective criteria. I knew others had received better terms for generally similar work; however, I did not know who, specifically, had received more, how much they received, and just what work they performed."[4]

Meyer's efforts had some impact. The dean responded, offering a salary increase of 50% provided that Meyer teach an additional three-credit course. The dean also offered to provide an additional round trip airline ticket. Meyer agreed, with no further negotiation. While Meyer might have been able to bargain for more, the raise to $15,000 and the added course served his monetary and nonmonetary interests well: more work, more pay, more effective use of his time – and he was very happy to keep teaching in the program. The additional plane ticket served both sets of interests as well, because Meyer was now able to fly home to spend time with family in the middle of the semester without reducing his income from the engagement.

Meyer greatly enjoyed the stay in Turkey and the courses he taught allowed him to experiment and develop as a teacher. He used his time out of the classroom developing new teaching material, reading every book the library had to offer on negotiation and conflict resolution, and dipping his toe into the waters of writing for publication.

The next year, Meyer was invited once again, and this time he agreed to come without requesting any monetary changes to the arrangement. He did take care to note to the dean in his acceptance that this might not be his response in the future. Instead, Meyer asked for other things of value to him, including an adjustment to the course schedule allowing him to take a week off in the middle without extending the overall duration. The dean agreed, allowing Meyer to break his stay down into two chunks of 4–5 weeks each, with about 10 days at home in the middle. Not only did the semester go well, but Meyer's time at home greatly improved the overall experience.

The next year, Meyer once again received a contract in the mail and, once again, he crossed out the number and made some changes. In an email Meyer explained to the dean that he would require a higher salary in order to continue teaching the next fall. The "objective criteria" he used as an explanation were not necessarily criteria, nor necessarily objective, but they were very real to him, and hard to objectively *deny*: his family was growing (his third child was on the way) and costs were rising.

After a period of silence, the dean wrote back to Meyer, saying he might be able to raise the salary by interesting the university's business school in a negotiation course for its MBA program. When Meyer expressed interest in principle, the dean wrote back offering a raise of $2,500 to teach a 1.5-credit MBA course. This sum was justified, he explained, given its proportionality to the previous raise of $5,000 to teach a three-credit course.

While it was unclear whether the dean was negotiating on behalf of the business school or negotiating with the business school on Meyer's behalf, it served Meyer well. On the one hand, Meyer did not have a relationship with the business school, and had he negotiated directly with them, he would have needed to start everything anew. The dean had marketed Meyer's teaching skills and obtained an offer. On the other hand, Meyer recognized that this structure also cornered him into accepting the objective criteria of the value-per-credit set in previous negotiations, which now worked against him. He didn't have any good reason to buck that standard of precedent, and in the context of the relationship Meyer and the dean now had, using unsound arguments could have more potential for harm than benefit. As Meyer confessed, "I realized I had been a partner in cornering myself, and while I could have just said no, I decided to enjoy the extra money, the challenge of teaching in a new disciplinary field, and the learning that would come with that."[5]

While Meyer ultimately accepted the standard, he pointed out to the dean that there was now another stakeholder involved, and perhaps the business school could provide funding for an additional plane ticket home during the semester. This served Meyer's interest of being home more and was a very "yesable" proposition for the business school, as they were used to bringing in experts from abroad and internalizing the cost of their travel.

Finally, Meyer also asked the dean to compress his teaching semester even further, into eight weeks, in order to be with his growing family. It was hard for the dean to say no to this, particularly since Meyer had accommodated his financial offer. Overall, Meyer's family interests were served, the dean gained favor with the business school, and the university's overall costs were only lightly impacted.

Lessons Learned

This case brings together many useful lessons to consider, including who gets to set the agenda in a negotiation and how, the importance of objective criteria, the role of cultural norms, and the importance of building the relationship in order to create better deals in the end.

Lesson 1: Presentation and Authority Matter in Nudging People in Certain Directions

How things are presented to people matters a lot and can sub-consciously move negotiators in certain directions. As Meyer mentioned, each year he was mailed a contract to sign. This contract had everything filled in, was printed on thick expensive paper, on university letterhead and with the special letterhead of the president's office in gold ink. In fact, the president of the university had already signed the contract.

Each year, as Meyer changed wording, crossed things out and sent it back, he thought it was a shame that they had gone to all that effort when it would have been so much easier to be in touch ahead of time for a discussion. Perhaps, as Meyer thought, they were trying to make things as simple as possible, given the distance?

It was only after three or four years of teaching that Meyer mentioned this process to a fellow faculty member at the university. "Yes, they do it that way for me as well. That's how they do it for everybody." Meyer was surprised. What a wasteful way to do things, he thought. "But don't you feel bad," he asked, "when you mark it up and send it back, or go into the dean for a talk to ask him to update your salary and send you a new contract?" Meyer's colleague was taken aback. "Mark it up? I just sign it and hand it in at the office. That's what everybody does!"[6]

This was a lightbulb moment for Meyer. The contract was psychologically influencing the professors, on behalf of the dean, by making negotiation seem laborious ("You're going to ask them to print up a new contract?"), costly ("You want them to scrap a document with gold ink on it? That must cost four thousand dollars an ounce"), wasteful ("That paper is so thick and sturdy! If you make them print out a new contract, you're passing a death sentence on four trees."), and disrespectful ("You're going to tell the dean that you expect him to go back to the president of the university and tell him, 'Professor so and so rejected the contract you signed for him the other day'?").[7] By contrast, just signing the contract was exceedingly easy. As a result, the dean spared himself the effort of dozens of contract negotiations every year, and the cost this would have incurred in raises. Simply by asking for more value, Meyer had taken himself out of the near-automated system of "contract renewal" for non-negotiators and placed himself in the dean's "contract negotiation" box.

Lesson 2: The Power of Framing and What Is Negotiable

The value of being the framer of the contract and the one to say, "I'll draft it" in contract negotiations, or "I'll write up a summary of our meeting," turns out to be subtly very valuable. This series of negotiations was also a lesson in how to set up offers or options while portraying them as non-negotiable, seemingly an objective criterion justifying themselves, even though they are nothing but one side's offer or request. Many systems are built around the fact that most people will simply not actively attempt to change an offer; they will either take it or leave it. In cases where those few people do ask, though, there is often room for negotiation and finding value.

Lesson 3: How Having and Using Objective Criteria Can Be Key to a Negotiation

Objective criteria can be essential to effective negotiation. As Meyer explained, early on in this negotiation process he had no objective criteria in the form of an industry standard pay scale and it really hampered him in his first negotiation. As a result, he very likely worked for less than he should have. However, as time wore on Meyer grasped the importance of this and used more objective criteria to make his case. This ultimately helped him to negotiate more effectively in the long run.

Lesson 4: One Negotiation Leads to Another – with Unintended Benefits

The negotiations Meyer had initially with the dean lead to an entry into the business school and another set of negotiations. When the business school asked Meyer, several years after he had left the conflict resolution program, to teach a negotiation course in the weekend executive MBA program, he was able to unhook his pay scale from everything that had been done before, and reset the process. This time around, with the course no longer framed as a discounted add-on course, Meyer supported his request with suitable standards of salary, and the business school administrators had no reasonable reason to turn down his proposal. Valuing the relationship, they did not even try to bargain the price down, and paid it willingly. In return, Meyer was happy to accommodate certain scheduling requests the school posed to him.

Lesson 5: Relationships Are the Oil That Greases the Wheel of Negotiation

As Meyer shared, "Relationship can make people do things that a million words in a contract would not."[8] The relationship between Meyer and the business school evolved with every respectful and mutually successful contract negotiation. The strength of this relationship withstood not only negotiation over the stickier points of some contractual issues, but also two other significant incidents.

The first event occurred when Meyer decided to postpone completion of a course, given a dramatic spike of conflict between Turkey and Israel that caused him to feel unsafe in Turkey. The business school supported Meyer in his decision, despite the inconvenience it caused to the school and the students, and received him warmly when he returned several months later to complete teaching the course.

Several years later, Meyer was on campus teaching a weekend course when a dramatic, frightening, and violent event happened during the night between his two classes: an attempted coup and its swift and decisive suppression. Out of commitment to the students and the institution, Meyer taught his class the next day, providing a supportive environment of sorts to students whose minds were still reeling from the events. Moreover, Meyer returned to Turkey the next weekend to complete the course as planned. He did this despite the deteriorating security situation and a spate of trip cancellations by other teachers, businesspeople, entertainers, and diplomats.

Reflecting on this, Meyer appreciated the generative connection between negotiation and relationship. "Our relationship developed with each negotiation. By the time we hit real-life situations that nobody would ever anticipate in a contract, our relationship was strong enough to fill in the blanks."[9]

Notes

1. Interview with Noam Ebner.
2. Interview with Noam Ebner.
3. Interview with Noam Ebner.
4. Interview with Noam Ebner.
5. Interview with Noam Ebner.
6. Interview with Noam Ebner.
7. Interview with Noam Ebner.
8. Interview with Noam Ebner.
9. Interview with Noam Ebner.

Conclusion

"The best way to show that a stick is crooked is not to argue about it or to spend time denouncing it, but to lay a straight stick alongside it."

– D. L. Moody[1]

This book has set out to do what Mr. Moody suggested. Instead of telling people the value of negotiation, I sought to show them its usefulness through a series of real-world negotiation examples. Through the use of case studies, the reader might easily envision not only that the difficult problems herein could be solved, but also *how* the negotiators involved went about solving them. This demonstrative approach was necessary because when the average person thinks about negotiation, they conceptualize the process with a very limited view of its utility. However, after reading the cases in this book it should be very difficult to maintain this perspective.

The case studies themselves were laid out in a fashion that generally mirrors how negotiations often unfold. The cases began with background and the preparation the parties engaged in. The preparation phase is an absolutely critical aspect of any negotiation and one in which people do not spend nearly enough time. After the preparation phase, the parties come together – often on multiple occasions – to try to solve a difficult problem or to work on a deal that will benefit them. That is followed by the implementation of the deal and the lessons that the parties learn after the fact that they must manage as the process unfolds.

Threads: The Five Principles That Make Negotiators Great

While each of the cases yield specific lessons, from improving one's BATNA to managing cross-cultural challenges, important core elements run through all the cases. The five principles mentioned at the outset of the book are reiterated again below because they make great negotiators, well, great. Specific cases are highlighted that reveal each of the principles in action.

Principle 1: Preparation

As the reader will have seen across all the cases, the parties engaged in significant preparation. The parties did their homework on their own approach and core interests, background research on the other parties and their needs, and on the situation in general and critical dynamics to consider. This preparation helped the negotiators to notice opportunities and to view the process differently in constructive ways. Recall a few examples of how preparation proved to be vital for creative solutions to emerge.

In the case about the sole supplier in China, and the need to negotiate a reasonable price for a piece of equipment (Chapter 9), preparation proved to be the essential ingredient to success. Working with the Innoagri team, the consultant gave them the significantly challenging task of improving their BATNA by imagining the sole supplier, Solantar, had gone out of business. To improve their BATNA they spent three days researching and thinking differently about the negotiation problem in front of them. In the end, they were able to come up with an approach that leveled the playing field and enabled them to negotiate more effectively with Solantar.

The example from Germany about the sale of the famous DEFA movie studio (Chapter 13) also illustrated the critical nature of preparation. The French company, CGE, that was interested in buying the movie company had to conduct extensive research and understand some of the critical interests of the German company, AT. Without intricate knowledge of their needs and the non-negotiables involved, an agreement would have proven elusive.

Finally, ponder the example of the recycling company Rambling Recyclers, which had to serve as an agent and negotiate on behalf of a much bigger company, Savory Grain Products (Chapter 7). Rambling Recyclers had to find the right balance between not only negotiating with AL Recovery, Savory Grain Product's previous supplier, but also redefining the broader relationship. Had Rambling Recyclers not done their homework, understood what was valuable to AL Recovery, and been prepared to temporarily walk away, they would not have been able to develop a lasting relationship with AL Recovery built on mutual long-term interests.

Principle 2: Mindset and the Importance of the Relationship

The second principle that was evident from the cases was the importance of a negotiator's mindset. There was ample opportunity for the parties in all these cases to bring a win-lose approach to the table. However, the parties resisted that, and instead brought a mutual gains outlook. This was not easy to do when the pressure was on and the consequences were great. Here is a reminder of a few cases in particular where mindset was fundamental to success.

The case of the two nonprofit entities – Life Care International for the Benefit of Children (LCIBC) and Life Care International (LC) – with similar names (Chapter 25) is a terrific example of a mindset problem. While both entities were very willing to solve the problem, they initially became stuck in a legal framework that seemed to limit their creative thinking. Only when the parties sought out a mediator who thought differently and questioned certain assumptions were the parties able to break the deadlock. The mediator's simple yet keenly insightful question proved to be the shift the parties needed to solve the matter.

The example of the executive of Ecru, a small clothing company in New York, who traveled all the way to India to secure a deal with Indegopro (Chapter 17) demonstrates the value of emphasizing the relationship. While Indegopro technically was considerably more powerful, they ultimately took a collaborative approach to the negotiation because they witnessed a herculean effort on the part of Howard Sheer, the CEO of Ecru, to reach a deal. His commitment and investment in the relationship proved to be a gesture that encouraged a certain mindset and fostered a cooperative approach.

Finally, the example of a small engineering firm, Contrexo, that broke away from its parent company, Mantosar, shortly after being acquired (Chapter 5) had all the makings of a lawsuit and a disastrous costly divorce. As the parties tried to find their way through a series of minefields, they fell back on the close relationship between the principals. Literally on the back of a cocktail napkin the negotiator's leaned on the relationship and shifted their mindset to a mutual gains approach and ultimately a deal.

Principle 3: Creative Problem Solving

While virtually every case in this book is steeped in creative problem solving, some of the negotiations would never have gotten anywhere without this attitude. These cases could easily have degenerated into a positional battle with the other being seen as an adversary and an impediment to success. The parties in all these cases resisted that trap and came out achieving their objectives.

Consider the complicated scenario from Afghanistan (Chapter 19). A United Nations human rights team was confronted with a unique challenge based on some initial information that was dubious, at best. However, as the United Nations team followed the evidence, they determined that a group of women were indeed being held against their will and being used in deeply inappropriate ways. What to do at that point was not an easy decision – particularly with over twenty lives hanging in the balance. Instead of taking a divisive stance toward the other party, despite the temptations, the team recognized the need to engage in creative problem solving and to give the perpetrators a face-saving way out. Without that approach, the women almost surely would have been condemned to a tragic fate.

Shifting to Canada, the Canadian company CXX that sought to develop a device that used laser technology (Chapter 16) was faced with a very difficult decision. The project was not unfolding in the way that CXX had imagined. CXX could have fired the Chinese company, Manufix, and started over. Instead however, CXX put on their collective creative problem-solving hat and brought in another complementary firm, Lazo, to do the work Manufix could not succeed in managing. As such, CXX met their goal of getting the project done on time and enabled all the parties to save face and prosper.

Similarly, recall the example of DOAR, which works with law firms to provide expert witnesses for large court cases (Chapter 6). A legal issue related to indemnification arose with the law firm Pine and Whitney, which wanted to hire an expert through DOAR. As the parties became entrenched, a closer examination of DOAR's BATNA revealed a way out of the conundrum. Through creative thinking DOAR was able to connect the expert directly with Pine and Whitney and then create a side deal with the expert so they still gained from the agreement. It was a triple win that arose out of the ashes of a collapsing deal.

Principle 4: Managing the Emotional Side of Negotiation

As has been previously discussed, one of the aspects that makes negotiation most difficult is managing the emotional side of the process. As many have recounted, if emotions could be taken out of negotiation the process would be much simpler. But that, as you now know from all of these cases, is impossible. The key, as my colleague William Ury likes to say, is to learn to manage the emotional elements and have your emotions with some control or they will have you. When your emotions have you, they overwhelm you and impact the process in an unproductive and self-defeating manner. Conversely, when the negotiating parties learn to manage their emotions productively, good things happen.

Recall the case of Diniz and Naouri – two billionaires who had been embroiled in a high-stakes international business negotiation that resembled a brutal and costly tug of war (Chapter 10). As the negotiation began to break down and move into the public realm, the situation quickly escalated out of control. Much of that intensification was fueled by insults and negative emotions that got the better of the two men. Enter Ury, who focused his attention not on the substance but on the emotionally laden issues connected to the men's respective underlying needs. Once those needs were out on the table, Ury was able to move the parties into a different and more productive place. Freedom and dignity, which had been trampled upon in the negotiation, became positively construed. The sense of relief was palpable because those needs were finally met. A deal was done as a result.

Another example where managing emotions effectively lay at the heart of the negotiation was the hostage case between Bill, the hostage taker, and Nicole, the hostage negotiator and her broader team (Chapter 23). In that example Bill was angry about many things and focused his ire on law enforcement and governmental institutions. His rage and frustration were profound.

Nicole was able to connect with Bill emotionally in an effective manner that gave him the opportunity to vent his feelings without hurting anyone. Once he had done that and Nicole refrained from judging him, the negotiation changed. Nicole was able to take Bill to the balcony and get him to come out from behind his barricade. How emotions were managed in this instance was critical and a valuable lesson for us all.

Finally, think back to the negotiation between the father, Marcel, and his son Louis, that transpired in a country in Europe (Chapter 15). The negotiation was over succession and the terms under which Louis would enter the family business. The negotiation had bogged down badly due to many years of problems that were burdened with emotional baggage. After a consultant entered the picture, he was able to help the father and son manage the emotional elements involved and discuss the underlying issues giving rise to these challenges. Once they were able to get to that level and addressed the emotions involved, they were more comfortable negotiating an arrangement that met their needs.

Principle 5: Uncovering the Hidden Dimensions of Negotiation

Underpinning literally every case in this book, and a key to their success, is the concept of getting down to the hidden dimensions of negotiation and the underlying interests of the parties involved. Without deciphering what is really happening under the surface, a negotiator is missing vital information that often holds the secret to progress. Consider these examples that relied largely on understanding the hidden elements of the negotiation.

The first case study that hinged on uncovering hidden dimensions and underlying interests had to do with Iron Works, the company in the Middle East that produces aluminum, and the Seabourn Trading, the shipping company that delivers the raw material from afar (Chapter 11). In the negotiation itself, Iron Works uncovered a few different hidden elements to the negotiation, including a very prosperous back haul that Seabourn Trading was enjoying. Once Iron Works discovered this dimension of the relationship, the power dynamic between the parties changed instantly. Furthermore, Iron Works learned of some potential misdoings on the part of Seabourn Trading, which further nudged the parties closer toward a solution. Without these two issues coming to the surface, a new deal likely would not have emerged.

The second case that demonstrated a heavy focus on underlying issues was the cross-cultural encounter between Kyammi, the South Korean company, and Bundascorp, the German company (Chapter 18). In this instance the hidden dimension was culture and the expectations that went along with appropriate responses in a negotiation. Sadly, these hidden aspects remained that way – ultimately leading to an agreement, but not one that was as productive as possible for both sides. Had those cultural norms been unearthed and understood by Bundascorp, the negotiation might have indeed ended differently, with both sides more satisfied.

The last case whose success relied on grasping the hidden dimensions of the negotiation was the scenario between two companies that merged. In that example, Amity and Branco had merged, but had not done so on equal footing (Chapter 2). As the details of the post-merger reality began to take hold, an unexpected change came about. Amity decided to tax each division in a new way that would cost Branco a significant sum of money. According to Amity, the tax was supposed to cover the costs of harmonizing the two firms' computer systems and other technologies. The more dire the situation became, the more panic set in. That is, until one employee from Branco looked below the surface and found an innovative solution based on the underlying interests of the parties.

Putting It All Together

While there is no guarantee these five principles alone will foster success in *every* negotiation, they certainly give negotiators a much better chance to achieve their goals than if they are not done. As the reader has likely learned from the cases, there are knowns and unknowns when it comes to negotiation. In general, I like to follow the 80% to 20% rule in my negotiations that I learned from my colleague Michael Wheeler from Harvard Business School. I believe I can understand approximately 80% of what is likely to transpire if I am really well prepared. That leaves roughly 20% of the negotiation that I have to react and adapt to as it unfolds. As has been discussed throughout the book, this is due to the reality that we are always working with incomplete information in our negotiations.

That stated, the case studies in the book demonstrate that effective negotiation happens in a multitude of different ways. Often the most improbable of negotiation solutions occur in the face of tremendous odds through creativity and persistence. These breakthroughs occur when a negotiator is thinking that a solution is simply not possible, or they have run into what seems like an insurmountable obstacle. But they don't quit. Their desire to find a solution, and belief that one can be found, is essential to their success.

My advice to you as you go forward is rather simple and can be summed up in two straightforward phrases. Be endlessly creative. Never give up.

Note

1. From https://www.goodreads.com/quotes/198756-the-best-way-to-show-that-a-stick-is-crooked

Glossary

In order to think through the lessons from these cases most effectively, you will need to know the definitions of some core negotiation concepts (listed in alphabetical order below). Many of these may be familiar to you; others may be new.

Agent

A person or entity who acts for, or in place of, another individual or entity as their representative in a negotiation with another party. An agent can have either full or limited authority to act on the behalf of the party they represent.

Alternatives and BATNA (Best Alternative to a Negotiated Agreement)

Alternatives are all of the actions a negotiator might take if they cannot reach an agreement with the other parties to a negotiation. A negotiator might have a number of alternatives in a given negotiation. When a negotiator does have multiple alternatives, it is important to determine which of those is the best. That best alternative is known as a Best Alternative to a Negotiated Agreement (i.e. BATNA or walkaway alternative). BATNA helps a negotiator to compare different pathways in front of them and what their best course of action is in a given situation. A key element of BATNAs is that they are in no way reliant on the other negotiator.

Anchoring

Anchoring is an effort to frame a negotiation around a certain reference point so that the conversation will proceed from that place forward. Anchoring is closely connected to first offers (see below) because anchoring most often occurs at the outset of a negotiation.

Aspiration point

An aspiration point in a negotiation is an inflated point that a negotiator may begin with in order to make concessions. An aspiration point would be the ideal that a negotiator might achieve in any negotiation.

Concessions

Concessions are tradeoffs made in negotiation. Concessions are about yielding or compromising on issues involved in a negotiation with the intention of helping a negotiator reach agreement.

Distributive negotiations (aka Positional negotiations)

A distributive negotiation is a competitive strategy in which one party gains at the expense of the other. The process is often focused on a single issue to be negotiated, typically involves price, and is heavily geared to bargaining and haggling.

Expanding the pie

Expanding the pie is a metaphor for creating value in negotiation. In every negotiation there is a "pie" of resources that ultimately needs to be divided. If negotiators can understand what the others value in a negotiation they can expand the pie before dividing it – thereby giving all involved a bigger piece.

First offers

First offers are the initial proposals one negotiator makes to another. While the concept is fairly straightforward, whether a first offer should be made or not is a topic of much debate. Some negotiators take an *always* or *never* approach to first offers. Those that *always* make first offers are trying to frame the negotiation on their terms. Those that *never* make first offers are trying to gather information and determine the parameters of negotiation.

Framing

Framing is a certain perspective, or way of setting up a negotiation, where specific elements of the process are emphasized to one's benefit. Framing is also about setting the agenda and trying to determine what issues the negotiation will focus upon.

Going to the balcony

Going to the balcony, first discussed in Ronald Heifetz's book *Leadership Without Easy Answers*, means to step back from a situation to take a big picture view. This is often done to get perspective on a situation but also importantly to manage the emotional aspects of a negotiation.

Integrative negotiation (AKA principled negotiation or interest-based negotiation)

Integrative negotiation is an approach taken most often when there are multiple issues to be discussed and there is typically a long-term relationship between the negotiating parties. Integrative negotiation, as its name suggests, seeks to integrate the goals of all the parties through understanding underlying interests and engaging in creative problem solving.

Interests

Interests underlie positions and are the "why" beneath the "what" in negotiation. Interests are often viewed as the hidden motivations for people in negotiation. Interests often lie under the surface of a negotiation and require exploration to uncover them. Interests can be either tangible (i.e. budgets or money) or intangible (i.e. concepts such as respect or face saving).

Logrolling

An exchange that involves making negotiation concessions by trading off issues so each party can try to maximize their value. Party A offers Party B something that Party B values more than Party A. In exchange, Party B reciprocates in a similar fashion.

Mediation

Mediation is often referred to as assisted negotiation. Mediation is a process where a third party tries to help the parties to a conflict to negotiate a solution. While there are many different types of mediators, the most common type in the United States is one who is focused on process and helping the parties find a solution themselves. Mediators are typically seen as impartial in their views and approaches to the conflict.

Negotiation styles

Negotiators have different styles that they use to approach their negotiations. The five typical styles are competing, avoiding, compromising, accommodating, and collaborating. Most people have a primary style and then one or two other styles that they can shift to depending on the other negotiator(s) they are dealing with and their style.

Objective criteria (aka external criteria)

These are factual data or examples that negotiators refer to that are outside of the current negotiation. Objective criteria, such as precedent-setting examples from similar situations, industry or market standards, the law, or scientific judgment, can help the parties to gauge a situation in front of them or assist them in finding a solution based on these external measures.

Options

Options are the creative solutions that negotiators generate together during the negotiation process. While options can certainly be developed by one negotiator on their own, most successful options are created jointly by all the negotiators involved. This creates ownership in the proposed solution. Options are a result of creative thinking. The best options seek to maximize the value in any negotiation.

Positions

Positions are what someone wants in a negotiation. Positions are the things people directly ask for in a negotiation and serve as a statement of need.

Power asymmetry

A power asymmetry in negotiation is where one party has more negotiating power than the others. Power is a more nuanced concept in negotiation than in general because it is relational in nature (i.e. one negotiator has to value what the other negotiator has in order for that negotiator to have power over them).

Reservation point

A reservation point is the least favorable deal that is acceptable
to a negotiator. Put differently, a reservation point is the line
not to cross and under which a deal no longer makes sense for
various reasons. The reservation point is strongly linked to the
concept of BATNA that was previously mentioned.

Target point

A target point is the place in a negotiation where a negotiator is
desirous of ending up after concession making. It is the point where
a negotiator really wants to be at the culmination of the process.

Three means of persuasion: ethos, pathos, and logos

In his treatise *Rhetoric*, written 2,300 years ago, Aristotle laid out
the three means of persuasion: ethos, pathos, and logos. Ethos
is the credibility and trustworthiness that a negotiator possesses.
Ethos is about why someone should listen to a negotiator in a
given context. Pathos is about the emotional connection or bond
that a negotiator builds with the other negotiator. Pathos is about
relatability. Finally, logos is about the logic that a negotiator
uses to make their case to the other. Taken together, these three
means of persuasion form a very powerful overall approach.

Zone of Possible Agreement

The Zone of Possible Agreement (ZOPA) is a zone in negotiation that determines if there is overlap between what the negotiators want/need. If there is overlap in the ZOPA then there is
a high likelihood of success. If there is no overlap in the ZOPA
then a deal is less likely and requires creativity to bridge the
gaps in the negotiators' positions.

Acknowledgments

This book could not have been done without the support of my family. My wife, Adina, and my children, Kayla, Aylee, and Talya, all kept me going and helped in only the way a close-knit family can. Your laughs and love fuel me, but also nudged me along slowly but surely when I struggled. My parents, Earle and Vicki Weiss, instilled in me a love of learning and a drive to succeed. My life and career would not be where it is today without their guidance, devotion, and encouragement. My sister, Ilana, has provided me with an undying level of support over these many years. It has been so very valuable to me and a source of great comfort when I need it most.

Also not to be forgotten is my extended family, who provided valuable ideas and feedback on the book: Mark Elfant, Wendy Schofield, Mary Jane Elfant, Adam Elfant, Susan and Barry Levant, Jared and Shaleah Levant, Jeremy and Rachel Matthies, Rebecca Levant and Nir Sadger, Sarah Levant and Yair Taylor, Robert Cohen, and David Lithwick.

To my dear colleague and friend William Ury: Words will not do justice to the profound gratitude I have for you with regard to this book, but more importantly, for all you have done for me over the course of my career. You have been an amazing mentor who helped me to grow and evolve. You knew when to nurture me and when to let go and push me to the forefront so I could be challenged, could succeed, and sometimes fail. Most of all, you have tried harder than anyone I know to live the principles of interest-based negotiation and successful conflict resolution. You show the way, not only through your words, but also through your deeds. As I have learned over the years, this is one of the hardest things to do in life.

Many other professional friends and colleagues provided me with valuable feedback and ideas along the way. These esteemed individuals include Brian Blancke, Seth Freeman, David Hass, Sheila Heen, Liza Hester, Jerome Bellion-Jourdan, Thomas Loper, Melissa Manwarring, Timothy Murray, Joe Navarro, James O'Brien, James Sebenius, Daniel Shapiro, Robyn Short, Ivan Shouker, Douglas Stone, Anthony Wanis St. John, Stefan Szepesi, Scott Tillema, and Michael Wheeler.

This book would simply not have been possible without all the contributors of the case studies. I am deeply indebted to my friends and colleagues for entrusting these stories to me and helping me to understand the nuances involved in each case. For confidentiality purposes I cannot list them all here individually, but this book would not be in your hands without them.

Finally, I would be remiss if I did not thank all the people I have trained and my many students over the years. You have taught me as much about negotiation as I have taught you. Your constant challenging and thoughtful questions have pushed me to think and grow with you.

About the Author

Dr. Joshua N. Weiss is the co-founder of the Global Negotiation Initiative at Harvard University and a senior fellow at the Harvard Negotiation Project. He is also the director and creator of the Master of Science degree in Leadership and Negotiation at Bay Path University in Massachusetts. Finally, he is the president of Negotiation Works, Inc. – a leadership, negotiation, and conflict resolution consulting firm.

Dr. Weiss received his Ph.D. from the Institute for Conflict Analysis and Resolution at George Mason University in 2002. In his current capacity he conducts research; consults with many different types of organizations; delivers leadership, negotiation, and conflict resolution trainings and courses; and engages in negotiation, mediation, and conflict resolution efforts at the organizational, corporate, government, and international levels.

Dr. Weiss's previous books include *The Negotiator in You* paperback book, audiobook, and ebook series, and a children's book series designed to teach children ages 6 to 10 about conflict resolution, negotiation, and problem solving. The series, *The Adventures of Emo and Chickie*, consists of three books and follows the adventures of these two friends as they try to help animals solve a difficult water conflict, assist a friend who is being bullied, and manage their way through a social media conflict.

Weiss is a member of the Program on Negotiation, Board Member of the Abraham Path Initiative, a global expert and specialist to the Mediation Support unit at the United Nations, and a board member of the World Affairs Council of Western Massachusetts.

Finally, Weiss delivered a *TEDx Talk* in 2018 entitled *The Wired Negotiator* about the role of technology in negotiation and how to use it most effectively.

Index

Page references followed by *t* indicate a table.